DESIGNING
AGAINST
VANDALISM

VNR **VAN NOSTRAND REINHOLD COMPANY**
NEW YORK CINCINNATI TORONTO LONDON MELBOURNE

Designing against Vandalism

First edition published in the United Kingdom 1979 by
The Design Council
28 Haymarket, London SW1Y 4SU

Published in the United States of America in 1980 by
Van Nostrand Reinhold Company
A Division of Litton Educational Publishing Inc
135 West 50th Street, New York, NY 10020, USA

Van Nostrand Reinhold Limited
1410 Birchmount Road, Scarborough
Ontario MIP 2E7, Canada

Edited by Jane Sykes
Designed by Michael McCarthy

Typeset by
Jolly & Barber Ltd, Rugby, England

Printed and bound in the United Kingdom by
A Wheaton and Co Ltd, Exeter

16   15   14   13   12   11   10   9   8   7   6   5   4   3   2   1

Contents

"The council were worried it might get vandalised"

Introduction

by Paul Burall, Design Council

The statistics on vandalism are depressing: the number of cases of criminal damage have risen dramatically over the years, reaching over 300,000 in England and Wales in 1978. The cost of vandalism is enormous too, the latest estimates being a minimum of £100 million a year. What is more, vandalism is not confined to slum inner city areas: Berkshire is a rich, largely rural, county, yet 269 of its 398 schools suffered from vandalism in one year at a total cost of £122,400.

But such statistics can mislead. For it is the distress caused to individuals that is the most pernicious result of the vandal's activities. A lift out of action in a high rise block can strand an elderly person or a mother with a young child; broken glass in the bottom of a paddling pool can badly gash a child's foot; vandalised street lighting can exacerbate traffic hazards and encourage thieves; and the general air of neglect created by graffiti, broken windows, and other signs of the vandal can be frightenening.

Indeed, combating vandalism was rated the most important priority in a survey of public opinion carried out by Merseyside County Council. Vandalism was ranked as more severe and more frequent than problems associated with public transport, homes, jobs, and some 20 other subjects.

Design has a key role in combating vandalism. First, designers can help to create an environment on a human scale that generates respect and a sense of belonging and thus discourages even thoughts of vandalism. In general, this means designing housing estates and public areas which are readily seen as belonging to individual people or families and which are obviously the responsibility of an identifiable local group of people. Vandals rarely attack property that appears to belong to someone who cares about it. There are numerous cases of empty houses left untouched for weeks or even for months but which, once one window is broken and not repaired, are rapidly and thoroughly vandalised.

People tend to respect an environment which is attractive and well maintained. There are many examples of this. For instance, one public building had no cases of vandalism in its well lit, pine-clad lifts until one of the lifts was temporarily lined with hardboard to prevent damage while moving bulky office equipment: graffiti started appearing almost immediately and soon covered the hardboard and other parts of the lift. Again, one effective answer to graffiti in subways – which are visually unattractive at the best of times – has been to decorate them with murals, often designed by local schoolchildren. It is also noticeable that decorative items that provide a focus and talking point for a community are rarely vandalised: thus standard street nameplates

The entrance to the car park at Greyfriars Shopping Centre, Ipswich, before it was decorated with murals

After decoration there has been no problem with graffiti

suffer from graffiti, but not the more decorative signboards used in some towns and villages.

Some vandalism can be traced back directly to poorly designed or badly made equipment. For instance, weak hinges or handles on entry doors to a block of flats inevitably suffer hard knocks: if they break, this may be classified as fair wear and tear, or it may be classified as vandalism; in either case, unless it is repaired rapidly, the breakage will signal neglect and quickly generate more deliberate vandalism.

The designer also has a role in making equipment and buildings reasonably resistant to vandalism. In some cases this can be achieved simply by siting vulnerable equipment out of the way: in a vandal-prone area, it may be advisable to site lighting control gear behind a wall or in an unobtrusive separate box rather than in the vulnerable base of the lighting column. In other cases, care can be taken to avoid using easily broken materials: glass panels at ground level in a school are almost certain to be broken, while overflow pipes jutting from the cisterns of a public lavatory are an invitation to vandals.

Some products – such as telephone boxes and cigarette vending machines – are natural targets for vandals whose motives often include petty theft. Here the designer can do much to deter the vandal by making the valuable contents of the equipment too difficult to reach even when attacked in a determined way. The Post Office faced major problems when decimal coinage dramatically increased the value of the contents of the average public telephone coin box, but careful design has now almost eliminated the problem. And the banks have had virtually no problems with their external cash dispensing machines.

Finally, the designer has a responsibility to minimise foreseeable consequent damage should vandals succeed in damaging equipment. Thus it is sensible to provide adequate drainage in a school lavatory block to cope with water from a broken tap or cistern. And concrete pipes in a playground for kids to crawl through should not be placed at the top of a slope, however firmly cemented into the ground they may appear to be.

Of course, design is only one part of what must be a comprehensive approach to tackling vandalism. The NACRO experiment in Widnes reported on later in this book demonstrates the importance of ensuring that designers and administrators do not impose solutions on people, but, instead, involve residents fully in making and implementing plans for their area.

Perhaps the most quantifiable success has been in the Gibbshill estate near Glasgow, where problems of crime and vandalism were once so great that shops resembled fortresses with bricked up windows and the Council even considered total demolition. Instead, with the full involvement of the tenants' association and the local police, the Council set about a dramatic £3 million environmental improvement scheme. More than 200 houses were knocked down to make way for amenities, including sports and recreation facilities, a community centre and a new shopping centre. The police reintroduced foot patrols and a local office, and even helped a local youth club by providing a hut. As a result, vandalism became almost non-existent and the number of crimes and offences dropped by almost 40 per cent at a time when the rate elsewhere was increasing rapidly.

More recently, an experiment by the Exeter Police Force has achieved considerable success, with an overall reduction of 14 per cent in juvenile crime throughout the city and a 40 per cent reduction in one high-crime area. The Exeter Police have achieved this by identifying high-crime areas, pointing out that these often coincide with areas with a lack of car ownership, little play space, and a population with low incomes, and then working with planners and other local authority staff in a joint effort to revive spirit in vandalised communities.

This book aims to help everyone concerned with tackling vandalism by bringing together a wide range of ideas and experiences and by offering some explanations for the motivation of vandals. The book stresses the essential link between the designers and architects responsible for creating the environment and the maintenance staff who gain a detailed knowledge of what goes wrong. It also offers advice about the kind of product to use in vandal-prone areas and highlights the criteria which should be applied to their design and construction.

There are no ready-made answers to all vandalism problems. Each problem and each area requires individual analysis and understanding. This book is intended to help that process and to suggest some of the possible choices which should be considered for action. But, perhaps more than anything else, the book stresses the importance of creating an environment in which individual people matter, for a neglected, graffiti-daubed concrete tower block estate conveys a feeling of contempt for the people who have to live there which itself generates either a lack of care or positive antagonism from those people.

The vandal's perspective: meanings and motives

by Robin Griffiths, lecturer in Criminology, Reading University, England and Assistant Professor of Law, New York Law School, USA
and Dr J M Shapland, Research Fellow in Criminology at the University of London, King's College

Destruction, defacement, breakage, graffiti, damage: what conduct should be considered vandalism? In this section we deal only with activity that falls strictly within the definition given in section 1 (1) of the Criminal Damage Act, 1971:

> A person who without lawful excuse destroys or damages any property belonging to another intending to destroy or damage any such property or being reckless as to whether such property would be destroyed or damaged shall be guilty of an offence.

It is, however, right to acknowledge at the outset that a great deal of such activity may not even be reported to the police, let alone recorded, so that official statistics of criminal damage fall far short of a full representation of the loss sustained by the community as a whole. Furthermore, people in certain positions in society may enjoy relative immunity from serious investigation or prosecution, given the circumstances in which their vandalism was committed. Thus, for example, university students during rag week and members of the armed forces after regimental functions have traditionally been allowed considerable licence; this may be especially true if the culprits can be relied upon to make good the damage afterwards.

It goes without saying that people's perceptions of the act of criminal damage will vary according to how they are involved. Plainly the perpetrator and the owner of the vandalised property are not likely to see it in the same way; but the police, courts and penal authorities will also bring their own particular perspectives to bear if the matter filters through to them. The media, who may or may not pick up a particular incident, can give events very different treatments depending very often upon the interest of the moment. (For example in 1976 it was soccer hooliganism.) The media are particularly prone to attach labels to vandalism such as 'senseless', 'malicious', 'thoughtless'.

This matter of perspective is important, and may be illustrated by the following passage:

A motorist pulled his car off a highway in Queens, New York to fix a flat tyre. He jacked up his car and, while removing the flat tyre, was startled to see his hood being opened and a stranger starting to pull out the battery. The stranger tried to mollify his assumed car-stripping colleague by telling him, 'Take it easy, buddy, you can have the tyres; all I want is the battery!'[1]

We shall concentrate here upon the perpetrator, the vandal himself. We are concerned to explore his attitude and motives as he engages in activity which falls within our definition as well as the contexts in which he may do so. We are not attempting to construct a typology of mutually exclusive categories of behaviour, and although we shall mention particular kinds of activity, we do not seek to suggest that any particular type is confined to the group we are then discussing.

The overwhelming majority of acts of vandalism are committed by the young, and many of these by the very young. It is true to say that the younger you are, the more likely you are to get caught, but even so it is quite startling to read Tony Marshall's findings[2] that when he investigated vandalism in Blackburn in the late 1960s the peak age for male offenders brought to the notice of the police was under 10. But this is not as surprising as it may appear at first sight when one appreciates that vandalism, despite its sinister connotations of the exercise of brute force upon the property of the defenceless, arises at that tender age from something almost universal – play.

Indeed, what we hope to demonstrate is that, generally speaking, motives and meanings change with age and context. The two are themselves linked because the kind of situation one finds oneself in may well depend upon one's age.

We will start at the bottom. Then, as Marshall suggests: 'It is part of all children's play to take things apart, climb trees, throw stones, or scribble on walls, and things naturally get damaged during such activity. This sort of damage is the predominant kind among children up to the age of twelve or so . . . Typically, a small group of boys is involved, many of them from areas not generally known for delinquency, and many of whom do not go on to commit any other crime.'[3]

Cohen writes:

In certain areas window breaking by small children during the course of a game (usually a competition to see who can break the most windows) is a highly institutionalized form of rule breaking. Derelict houses or houses under construction are usually chosen and other frequent targets are empty milk bottles and beer bottles. Such activity is usually not regarded as deviant simply because it is part of local tradition, or because the targets are regarded as 'fair game'.

GILLIAN DARLEY

Digging up a tree is play to these children, although the end result will be indistinguishable from deliberate vandalism

In the case of very young children, the damage might be accidental or the actors not thought old enough to understand the value of property. In any event the behaviour is seen as adventure, play or exuberance by both the actor and the audience, although neither, of course, need be totally unaware that what is being done might be looked upon as wrong or illegal.[4]

However, tolerance may be exceeded, for example, if the activity goes beyond a certain limit or if an inappropriate target is selected.

Vandalism as play often takes the form of a game of skill. As such, either the quantity or quality of the destruction is stressed. Wade has quoted one of a group of slightly older children (13- to 17-year-olds) he interviewed in Kansas City:

The first time we did vandalism, me and my brother and another boy down at the garage, we were smoking and playing cards. They had some old cars in the back; we played around there. We cleaned them out one day. Swept out the broken glass — busted windshields — rolled down the windows so we wouldn't cut ourselves. This one guy threw a whisky bottle up on the roof; threw another. It hit the side of the window. We just started throwing at the windows. When we were through, we'd broken 27 of them: we saw who could break the most. There wasn't anything else to do. We finally got tired and just left . . .[5]

DESIGN COUNCIL

This Mini is in a hospital car park. It is not clear who has vandalised it, but it could have been children playing or car strippers

Destruction, then, may be subordinate to the spirit of competition among participants as to who can achieve most, especially in hitting a target. However, once the spirit of destructiveness takes hold, it may then generate a momentum of its own. Predominately, though, the flavour of such childish activity is casual and spontaneous, and several researchers have remarked upon the importance of what Marshall calls a 'releaser' to create the spark which sets it off. A releaser is 'a cue in the environment which allows the offender to regard the act as not so serious or not important at all. This is why windows in empty houses so often get broken (especially in blocks which are believed to be waiting for demolition) or apparently abandoned cars are vandalized.'[6] In other words, the child is responding to the opportunity which presents itself for having a good time without any apparent owner or custodian to prevent him or complain.

The same goes for the next age group, roughly the 13- to 16-year-olds. But by now we have more factors at work, very much to do with the process of growing up. Play has receded in importance and is replaced by the importance of the opinion of a child's peers and his own self-esteem. The group now becomes a powerful focus of attraction and at the same time serves as the context in which status is acquired and must be maintained. Daring is an important ingredient in the search for prestige; so, too, is the creation of a posture of daring.

Whatever the individual's inner feelings, which may or may not favour a particular form of behaviour, the shared expectations of the group will exercise a considerable influence upon what he does and is prepared to do. These expectations will also be imputed to him by other members of the group so that it is possible for a situation to arise whereby each member of the group may himself be reluctant to engage in behaviour apparently demanded by certain opportunities and challenges, but his status in the group will forbid him to hang back.

It is not without significance that vandalism is one of the safest and most anonymous of offences. Rarely is there a personal complainant (since public property is such a ready target) and the offender does not have to carry away or dispose of property. Nor does he have to carry an instrument of destruction with him — simply hands or feet, or the use of an object lying ready to hand at the scene will often suffice. Since little is reported, few offenders are detected, which in turn affects the reporting rate. Unless the vandal is caught at the time, the chances of escaping detection altogether are extremely good.

Thus the potential cost of appearing to conform to the demands of the group by engaging in boisterous and sometimes obviously anti-social behaviour is probably at about its lowest where vandalism is concerned. Here again, at this age, we find the factors of tests of skill and competition but on a grander scale than with younger children. But the consequences are less easily tolerated by the social audience than when the perpetrators are younger. Hanging around in groups in the street, though inducing a feeling of security in the individual, also makes the group more visible to the outsider whose likely response is to feel threatened. The official reaction has an unfortunate knack of according the group a greater cohesion than it might otherwise possess: finding itself under attack, it closes ranks. Another noteworthy feature of the group context is the element of sheer excitement – almost a sense of abandon – whereby feelings of fear and guilt become engulfed in the sheer enjoyment of the moment.

At this age, criminal damage has a less widespread social incidence than it has at an earlier age. According to a recent Home Office Research Unit study by Francis Gladstone in Liverpool[7] some 30 to 40 per cent of his sample of secondary schoolboys engaged in such activity. Many of them admitted being involved in other types of delinquency as well, such as shoplifting and fighting. Vandalism to them is just part of the general pattern of street activity. It is worth stressing that it would be very rare to find someone whose only criminal activity was vandalism at this age. The persistent vandal has been shown[8] to be more likely to have committed offences of other sorts, to have come from a broken home and, if he has left school, to be out of work. It may be that, as Wade observed with his Kansas boys, once you are into a wider range of offences, property damage or destruction simply assumes a less serious image and may be undertaken more frivolously than hitherto.

The crime rate for boys in the late teens in general is beginning to fall off, and vandalism is no exception. By now, most boys are becoming distinctly interested in girls, some marry; and there are the demands of jobs. In other words, they find more areas of responsibility and there is more to lose by departing from conventional standards of conduct and having to suffer any official consequences. Again, it is more 'fun' and 'adult' to drink in a pub than to hang around on street corners, and for all these reasons the old 'peer' group becomes less attractive to its members than it used to be. The boys who remain in the group into their late teens are mostly those ill-equipped or hesitant to compete in the areas of activity to which their former companions have moved. These more disturbed, often aggressive, youths feel obliged to engage in more extreme forms of delinquency in order to maintain their dignity and indeed to justify their continued membership of the group. Vandalism by such perpetrators as these can be deliberately malicious and may be very costly to the victim.

This is not the only kind of property damage for which this age group is responsible. Increasingly prevalent by this stage is what is sometimes referred to as 'instrumental vandalism', that is damage done not as an end in itself, but as a step to achieving some other purpose, usually theft (from meters, telephone boxes or motor cars or by breaking and entering). Indeed, it is this kind of activity which accounts for the bulk of property damage done by adults. Though the label 'vandalism' is sometimes attached to the consequences, especially when the offender does not succeed in his primary motive (that is to say he does not actually steal anything), this vandalism is really no more than an incident in the perpetration of something quite different.

We should also consider a small group of types of vandalism whose motives and context are quite unlike those we have discussed so far. They are less common, and are confined to a comparatively small number of actors.

First, there is revenge against individuals or institutions. Here, not only is the destruction of property belonging to, or representing, the person or institution concerned in itself immediately gratifying, but it is also far safer than violence offered face to face with an individual. The perpetrator is also less likely to be arrested, tried or punished.

Secondly, there is vandalism as a result of general frustration or boredom where the vandal is hitting back at his general environment, especially at his school or at his place of work. Much industrial sabotage, which rarely gives rise to prosecution unless it goes beyond certain limits, falls into this category; it also serves to slow down the rate of production and hence to provide a temporary 'breather' from the demands of routine.

Thirdly, there is activity directed towards a specific end or for a particular cause. Political slogans, bill posting and certain activities of pressure groups, such as the 'Free George Davis' campaign (which gained considerable publicity by digging up the Test Match pitch at Headingley in 1975), fall into this category.

Finally we must mention the 'old lag', because he does a little damage from time to time, usually just enough to gain the attention he wants from the police to make them arrest him. This is a quixotic form of vandalism, because the aim will be to attract the attention of the authorities and so get a roof over his head for the night, even if it is a police cell, or even with a view to a further sojourn in prison when the pace of life outside has become unbearable.

The rest of this book considers vandalism as it occurs in different locations and as it affects different authorities. It must be remembered, however, that quite disparate motives and meanings in the minds of those responsible may serve to explain the incidence of apparently similar cases of damage. The preventive measures that may need to be taken to make any given environment vandal-proof may be different according to the nature of the vandal. It will be necessary to discover who the vandals are in any particular setting as well as the type of damage done. As an example of this, look at how a window in a deserted house may be broken. This may have been done by kids getting in to play; by older children as a game of skill; by adolescents or adults in order to remove the remaining furniture or fittings; by someone with a grudge against the present or previous landlord; by a pressure group to advertise the dereliction of empty property; or by an 'old lag' to gain attention or to doss for the night. Although the result is the same whoever broke the window, nothing else is.

The graffiti writer clearly considers that it is the Council that is guilty of vandalism

Notes

[1] Zimbardo, P: 'A field experiment in auto shaping' in Ward, C (ed): *Vandalism*, The Architectural Press (London 1973) p 90
[2] Marshall, T: 'Vandalism: the seeds of destruction', *New Society*, 17 June 1976 pp 625–627
[3] *Ibid* p 625
[4] Cohen, S, 'Property destruction: motives and meanings' in Ward, C (ed): *Vandalism*, The Architectural Press (London 1973) p 25
[5] *Ibid* p 47
[6] Marshall, T p 626 *op cit*
[7] *Ibid*
[8] *Ibid* and West, D J and Farrington, D P: *The Delinquent Way of Life*, Heinemann (London 1977)

Observations
on the nature of vandalism

by Sheena Wilson, a sociologist who as a member of the Home Office Research Unit undertook a three-year study of vandalism on London housing estates. She is now a Senior Research Officer with the Housing Development Directorate of the Department of the Environment. In this paper she expresses her personal views on vandalism.

Introduction

Formal methods of controlling vandalism, such as anti-vandal patrols, are unlikely to be truly effective since vandalism tends to occur just at the times of day when and in the places where the chances of its perpetrators being caught are minimal. Nor can the police play more than a limited part in tackling the problem as rates of reporting offences of criminal damage by the public are low;[1] reasons for this include the fact that much vandalism occurs in a piecemeal fashion with buildings and equipment being progressively damaged by a number of individuals, rather than in the form of identifiable single incidents. This section will be looking at some rather longer-term methods of tackling the problem, particularly at ways of motivating people not to commit acts of vandalism. It will also put forward a definition of vandalism which may provide some clues to how it may be prevented. The discussion is largely restricted to the context of public housing estates.

The arguments put forward here are twofold. The first is that vandalism has increased because there are now more opportunities for it to take place. The second is that the groups and individuals who commit most acts of vandalism are those who lack a sense of ownership and control over many aspects of their lives; what is needed therefore is for such people to have a greater degree of influence over their affairs.

The increase in vandalism is often attributed to the relaxing of standards of control and authority in the home, at school and at work. Since it would be unrealistic to try to reverse the broad trend of growing permissiveness, we have to explore ways in which people develop a sense of responsibility and consideration for others in the absence of more formal constraints on behaviour. This is particularly necessary in the context of cities.

As Jane Jacobs observed, cities are inhabited by strangers.[2] Informal processes of social control in cities cannot rely on those sanctions that exist in small and well established communities where everyone knows one another. City life has rather to depend on alternative sets of sanctions, at least where control of behaviour in public areas is concerned. These stem from such things as opportunities for surveillance afforded by street layout or patterns of use along a street, and from relationships of trust established between individuals through their functional interdependence. This applies equally in settings where the physical layout suggests that a self-conscious attempt has been made to recreate enclosed or 'village' communities within cities, for example on some housing estates. A city village differs from a traditional village in that the degree of mobility and cultural diversity within its population is likely to be high. Our methods of tackling vandalism therefore must be based on an understanding of how informal control mechanisms work amongst groups of strangers or in settings where relationships are usually impersonal.

Defining vandalism

Defining vandalism is difficult as it usually gains its meaning from the situations in which it occurs. To characterise it as an expression of aggression and destruction is not sufficient, since this does not distinguish it from other types of behaviour where these elements may also be present. It would be helpful perhaps to start by saying what it is not. For example, if someone breaks something, either accidentally or on purpose, and then proceeds to repair the damage, this is not generally seen as vandalism. If someone breaks something which belongs to him or her, or which has been discarded and so does not belong to anyone, the same applies. The label does not apply if things are broken in a context where 'letting go' is a legitimate activity, such as in an adventure playground. Finally, in some situations destructive activities are undertaken by a recognised authority and so are not seen as vandalism in the standard sense: for instance, when sound buildings are demolished in the course of municipal redevelopment.

From this at least three defining elements of vandalism can be drawn:

it is damage to things that are owned by someone (whether or not they are perceived to 'belong' to someone);

it is damage to other people's property;

it is damage that has to be mended by someone else.

Vandalism and opportunity

A Home Office study[3] has elaborated the point that much criminal or delinquent activity occurs because opportunities exist for it to do so. For example, it showed that rates of car theft fell once the installation of steering column locks on new cars became statutory, as this made theft more difficult and so somewhat diminished opportunity. The Oscar Newman thesis in *Defensible Space*,[4] which relates rates of crime to building design, is saying in essence very much the same thing: that is, that vandalism and crime occur where building design offers opportunities for such activities to take place by restricting surveillance of public areas, or reducing residents' ability to develop proprietary attitudes towards shared spaces.

Vandalism is commonly directed towards public property.[5] This is possibly because public property is not identified as belonging to anyone (although it does of course, but ownership is diffuse) and so acts of damage are seen as less reprehensible; also the likelihood of the perpetrators being stopped or caught is less, since public property does not receive the same degree of individual supervision as private property. There is a double-edged sense therefore in which public property is 'other people's'. An additional characteristic of public property is that 'other people' repair it.

Applying the 'opportunity' thesis with these points in mind, one factor contributing to post-war increases in vandalism is perhaps the very considerable increase in amounts of public property. Property in municipal ownership, including residential housing, schools, libraries, various other public buildings and open spaces, together with the offices from which these are administered, has expanded considerably since the war. Moreover, the equipment provided in all these settings is now more elaborate: for example lifts in public housing, gardens and street furniture, equipped play spaces, telephone kiosks, and the subways, footbridges and so on needed to separate pedestrians from motor cars. A physical world has developed of things that are public and that in general do not engender the attitudes of care and respect that private things do. Therefore a certain level of vandalism seems inevitable. This could be reduced to some extent if the way in which public property was designed and managed took full account of the fact public property carries a set of rules concerning its use and upkeep which differs from that which attach to private property.

What causes indifference?

A lack of care and respect does not necessarily lead to destructive attitudes, merely to one of indifference. However, when undertaking a study of vandalism on housing estates I often found it difficult to distinguish intentional forms of damage from wear and tear, indifference, neglect and thoughtlessness. Vandalism, it seemed, was part of a spectrum of behaviour which began with very common forms of carelessness, such as dropping litter, and continued through a wide range of rough handling – bumping prams into glass swing doors, taking short cuts through newly planted flower-beds – to the stage where damage became deliberate: glass broken by airgun pellets, smashed fittings and dismantled fire hoses.

It can be surmised that most of the people responsible for any of these forms of behaviour would not have behaved in the same way towards their own property, since it would be they, and only they, who would have to repair it or get it repaired. The dwellings themselves on highly vandalised council estates are usually very well looked after by their inhabitants. The ownership or possession of things because it carries with it this sort of responsibility may engender more general attitudes of care towards things in general, whoever they belong to. I am sure that the forms of indifference apparent in many acts of vandalism are most developed in those sections of the community that do not own or possess things and therefore have never had the responsibility of maintaining them. They are people who are never in the position of being depended upon or of being of consequence.

Ownership is a difficult term because of the emotive-political connotations attached to it, and its association with the legal sense of property ownership. Colin Ward expressed the meaning of ownership intended here by the phrase 'a sense of possession'.[6] Not only a thing but an activity or project, a person or place can be the object of a sense of possession. It means that a person can invest part of his or her identity in something or someone, and feel that actions he or she takes are of consequence; it means he or she has control over something and can

One tenant has erected a fence to create his own 'defensible space' in an area where tenants' territorial rights are not distinctively defined by the layout

either make something happen or stop it from happening. A group of children can feel that a play project 'belongs' to them in this sense, or tenants of rented property can make a space 'belong' to them. Legal property ownership is merely the most clearly defined form of possession and control, but it is certainly not the only one.

Developing responsibility

Children as a group generally have less property and fewer responsibilities than adults, and possibly for this reason are more prone to be vandals. However, contrasts between different groups of children, rather than children and adults, are also important. Non-achievers at school, children from very poor backgrounds, from broken homes, or from environments with little provision of play space and leisure activities – the groups that criminological literature commonly associates with high delinquency rates – are more likely to be deprived of any feeling of being of consequence or of having the welfare of an object or project dependent on them. They are less likely to develop an attitude of care for things because they have not experienced feelings of cherishing something of their own.

An unpublished study on train graffiti in New York[7] illustrates this point. Police officials, commenting on boys who regularly sprayed graffiti on underground trains, described them as 'nobodies trying to be somebodies'; they will sit for hours on a platform just waiting to see their name go by, and there is an accepted rule that no one writes over someone else's name.

This may be the only way Kenny's girlfriend feels he can assert himself

23

There are groups of adults, too, who have rarely or never experienced a feeling of being in possession or control. Deprived groups – those in a poor bargaining position for public housing, the unskilled in areas of high unemployment, families with multiple problems – are so described by virtue of the fact that they have very little control over their lives; and it is noticeable that they tend to guard jealously those few areas where they do have some control, for example where their children are concerned.

Vandalism and public housing

It is not within the scope of this book to discuss broad-ranging issues of unemployment and deprivation. However something will be said about public housing, especially as here it is possible to sound a note of optimism. There are many ways in which the management of public housing, and its design in the future, can be changed in order to give tenants a greater sense of control and responsibility (beyond purely token responsibilities exemplified by things like cleaning rotas for public stairways). These may help to modify the types of attitude, such as indifference or powerlessness, which contribute to vandalism.

What seems to be needed is a style of management which carries with it attitudes and expectations that imply that tenants are customers buying a service, not, as is often the case now, welfare supplicants. This applies to everyday transactions such as reporting repairs, rent queries and applying for transfers; a more relaxed atmosphere at the local housing office, an open and friendly manner on the part of housing officers, and less reliance on curt computer-printed communications could make a great deal of difference. More fundamental changes in the organisation and training of housing management may also be needed to bring about this different approach.[8]

At present attitudes of care and pride on the part of tenants are often expected to flourish in the barren wastes of public decks and pathways, the cleaning, repair and use of which are quite beyond the control of any one resident. Such attitudes are also expected in response to well meaning improvements made by housing departments who think they are doing things for tenants, when what tenants actually see are things being done to them.

An interesting controlled experiment in physical improvements on two similar 'cottage' estates, carried out by Oscar Newman in the United States, demonstrated this point (and there are many such examples in Britain too). At Clason Point Gardens, as reported in the book *Defensible Space*,[9] tenants were consulted and involved in the introduction of fairly minor physical modifications to the layout of their grounds; these proved to be a lasting success, with residents tending their gardens and taking more care of public areas too. In the other scheme, Markham Gardens, the improvements were provided in traditional management style: workmen simply appeared on the estate one day and started putting in fences and flower-beds. The response of the tenants was to rip up some of the fencing, which to this day merely provides obstacles to circulation to be removed or bent, rather than boundaries to private, owned spaces.

DESIGN COUNCIL

The treatment of this estate office might reflect the poor communication between management and tenants

DESIGN COUNCIL

Residents have made their own short cut on this London housing estate

The difficulties of achieving local participation and involvement should not be underestimated. It requires more than a few public meetings and the distribution of pamphlets. This conclusion arose from two experimental projects in Britain where environmental improvements were carried out in consultation with tenants. The two schemes took place on run-down estates in Oldham[10] and Widnes[11] respectively, the reports of which should be fruitful reading for any authority or group embarking on similar exercises, since in both cases vandalism decreased. In each project there was a need for regular personal contact between residents and officials. Initially a considerable gap existed in perceptions of the situation not only between officials and residents, but also between different groups of residents. Local authorities tend to consult a single tenant body, usually the tenants' association, because this is administratively convenient. However, it is unwise to assume that one small group of tenants is representative, or that all tenants' concerns are necessarily centred on the same things.

The style of housing management and the style of tenant consultation in public housing are both important aspects of a long-term approach to the prevention of vandalism. Physical modifications to buildings and equipment may appear attractive as more short-term solutions: these include both the measures suggested in *Defensible Space*, and vandal-proofing techniques to protect popular targets. This approach, however, is limited since it merely reduces opportunities for committing acts of vandalism rather than dealing with the motivation behind them; therefore it can only ever be a partial solution. Also, as Oscar Newman found, the way in which physical modifications are introduced is as crucial as the modifications themselves.

How to provide leisure facilities

Another element in the prevention of vandalism connected with housing concerns the provision of public play and leisure facilities; this is usually ill co-ordinated by local authority departments, although the lack of such facilities is often associated with the occurrence of vandalism. That these facilities are needed is argued elsewhere,[12] the points made here concern the form they should take, drawing from the experiences of several projects which aimed, amongst other things, to reduce vandalism.

The Exeter police force set up a small Crime Prevention Support Unit whose unique approach is currently being monitored by the National Association for the Care and Resettlement of Offenders.[13] The unit concluded, from a rigorous study of the location of reported offences and known offenders, that the way in which planners regulate the location of recreational facilities is highly inappropriate. Too often facilities are provided near the centre of town where transport links with major residential areas are poor; also the type of provision itself often requires considerable expenditure which is beyond the means of many children. A survey carried out by the unit showed that patterns of play for most children are highly localised, also that playing fields are infrequently used if these are flat and uninteresting. It is this sort of information that should be used as a matter of course to guide the planning and location of leisure facilities, but it rarely is.

It is often the case that facilities are not lacking, but are merely under-used, or children are not sufficiently encouraged to use them. The Exeter group managed to increase the number of children using one particular playing field from 10 to 300 within three weeks by turning up themselves to organise games of football. Following this success they persuaded local schools to open their grounds in the evening for children's use. The major problem they encountered in getting greater use made of local facilities, not necessarily just for schools, was in persuading people to bend the rules a little; often purely administrative objections were raised by officials who wanted to save themselves extra trouble and effort.

A major problem is that responsibility for children's leisure and recreation comes under so many different departments: leisure departments, parks and gardens departments, housing departments, and education authorities may all be involved, but there is rarely one officer to co-ordinate such provision. A major achievement of the Exeter Crime Prevention Support Unit was to take on this co-ordinating role; it was helped by the fact that the police have an established position of authority and a clearly defined role (although in this case they were extending it to unknown fields). Any local group concerned to reduce vandalism should perhaps start by looking into ways of co-ordinating responsibilities for provision of leisure facilities in order to maximise the use of those that already exist.

The contribution that leisure facilities can make to the prevention of vandalism is not simply as a diversion, a way of reducing boredom; it has been found in any case that play spaces are of little use in helping to reduce vandalism if they co-exist with equally diverting areas to play in, such as underground garages and lifts.[14] Their contribution lies rather in the attitudes of care, of self-importance, and of being depended upon which they can foster if organised in the right way. Projects which have had some success in reducing vandalism seem to be those with a creative element and which give a sense of possession and purpose to those taking part.

For example, a successful part of an anti-vandalism campaign organised by Halton local authority in 1975 was the painting of murals by groups of adolescents who then saw these murals as belonging to them and ceased to deface the walls they were painted on. A survey on one vandalised estate found that teenagers had never had their opinions asked of them before or been given tasks requiring responsibility; they did not get much pleasure from vandalism and particularly asked to be able to do positive things such as building their own shelter. (See the section on page 30).

A notable part of one conference on vandalism[*] was the appearance of three ex-vandals who explained that they had stopped smashing things after they had become involved with the urban farm organised by the Inter Action Trust in Kentish Town.[†] The farm, they said, had given them something to do that was 'interesting' and which they felt was theirs. On the farm responsibility is deliberately delegated to self-managing groups; the organisers also emphasised the practicality and stimulation to the imagination that the farm provides as contributions to its success.

There are many groups and organisations who could give the young practical and stimulating tasks relating to the upkeep and management of cities and not just to little rural enclaves carved out of derelict urban wasteland. As Colin Ward points out, recent city development has served to rob the young of their status.[15] It is time we found them a new role.

[*]Organised by the Conservative Central Office and taking place in November 1977.
[†]The Interaction Group who helped set up this farm, and others elsewhere, is sponsored by the Grants to Voluntary Bodies Unit of the Department of the Environment.

Notes

[1]Clarke, R V G (ed): *Tackling Vandalism*, HMSO (London 1978)
[2]Jacobs, J: *The Death and Life of Great American Cities*, Jonathan Cape (London 1961)
[3]Mayhew, P, Clarke, R, Sturman, A and Hough, J: *Crime as Opportunity*, HMSO (London 1975)
[4]Newman, O: *Defensible Space*, The Architectural Press (London 1973)
[5]See for example Ward, C (ed): *Vandalism*, The Architectural Press (London 1973) and *Wilful Damage on Housing Estates*, Digest 132, Building Research Establishment (London 1972)
[6]Ward, C: *Tenants Take Over*, The Architectural Press (London 1975)
[7]Cook, B: *A Look at Vandalism in the United States of America*, Central Office of Information (London 1977)
[8]Wilson, S and Burbidge, M: 'An investigation of difficult to let housing', Housing Review, July-August 1978

[9] Newman, O: *Defensible Space, op cit*

[10] Shenton, N: *Deneside — a Council Estate*, University of York (York 1976)

[11] Spence, J and Hedges, A: *Community Planning Project: Cunningham Road Improvement Scheme*, Social and Community Planning Research (London 1977)

[12] *Children at Play*, Design Bulletin 27, DoE (London 1972)

[13] Moore, C: *From Crime Statistics to Social Policies*, Devon and Somerset Constabulary 1978

[14] Wilson, S: 'Vandalism and design', *Architects' Journal*, October 1977

[15] Ward, C: *The Child in the City*, The Architectural Press (London 1978)

The Cunningham Road scheme

by Ann Blaber, formerly Crime Prevention Officer for NACRO, now consultant for the Department of the Environment on their Priority Estates Project.

The Cunningham Road scheme was initiated by NACRO (National Association for the Care and Resettlement of Offenders) and devised and carried out by SCPR (Social and Community Planning Research) and NACRO jointly.

Cunningham Road is a council housing estate in Widnes where an attempt to cut down vandalism seems to be working. Two years ago the estate was drab and the morale of the inhabitants was low. Now it looks cared for: people are doing their gardens, and say that it is a 'much nicer place to live'. The police say it has changed out of recognition, and there has been a 'dramatic decrease in crime'.

As Sheena Wilson suggests in the section on the nature of vandalism, there are basically two ways to set about trying to stop it: either you can try to prevent people from wilfully damaging their surroundings, or you can try to stop them from wanting to do so. To impose security to a degree where vandalism could be completely eradicated would not be practicable, and would probably not be acceptable in the social and political climate of Britain today. The alternative is arguably more difficult, but in the long run must be far more satisfactory.

The theory behind the Cunningham Road scheme is that if people like the place they live in and feel that it is theirs, they will want to look after it rather than destroy it. But how do you get people to feel like that about a council estate which has a bad reputation, is rundown and vandalised? The study set out to see whether people's attitudes might change if improvements were made based on their wishes and priorities, and if so, whether there would be less vandalism on the estate.

First we had to find a local authority prepared to test our ideas. Halton District Council were concerned about vandalism on estates, and realised they could do little about it without the co-operation of the tenants. It is important to stress the degree of co-operation and commitment of Halton Council, and to see any criticism of the Council within this context.

The Council selected the Cunningham Road Estate, with a population of approximately 1600, of which nearly half is aged under 17.

There were serious but not desperate problems. The houses are mostly two storey with front and rear gardens; 250 of them were built around 1950, and nearly 200 new houses and flats had just been built replacing prefabs, when the scheme started at the end of 1975. Most of the houses have three or four bedrooms, although the rooms and the gardens of the new houses are smaller.

When we started the older part of the estate was run down: a few houses were boarded up; others, though occupied, had broken windows. Most of the gardens were untended; fencing was a jumble of corrugated iron, wire and old boarding. The shops were barricaded with steel shutters, and daubed with graffiti. The streets were in poor condition, the pavements worse, and there were no trees in public places. Some of the houses are of concrete block construction, and were grey and streaked by nearly 30 years of pollution. There were signs of vandalism all over the old part of the estate: broken glass, graffiti on 'undefended' walls, smashed brickwork, and litter strewn around gardens, pavements and streets. The new part of the estate with its timber-clad and brick terraced houses and open-plan frontages looked much more attractive, but even there the playgrounds had been vandalised and the paving was littered with glass.

ALAN HEDGES

A graffiti-daubed fence on the Cunningham Road Estate

The residents had the reputation of being either apathetic or hostile. We were told by the Health Service that sometimes their staff had been too scared to get out of their cars; others said that many parents did not seem to care whether or not their children went to school; and the police suspected that there was more crime on the estate than was reported, some of which was thought to be self inflicted such as tenants breaking into their own meters. None of the authorities was optimistic about our (NACRO and SCPR) getting much co-operation from the tenants.

31

Our approach was influenced by the work of Oscar Newman, particularly in terms of the importance he attaches to a sense of control and ownership; but it differed in that our emphasis was on involving tenants through consulting them about their views, rather than on imposing our own preconceived ideas about the sorts of measures that should be carried out.

Public consultation has earned itself a poor reputation over the past few years, largely because it seldom amounts to more than a couple of public meetings and a few leaflets. As the scheme made clear, people who are not used to being consulted need encouragement to participate, they need to feel there is some point in bothering, and they also need time and assistance to analyse their problems and come up with considered views. It is only through discussion that people can start to recognise and manage the inevitable conflicts of interest and different points of view existing in any society; public meetings seldom provide a forum for such rational discussion.

SCPR devised a method of consulting tenants which provided an opportunity for people really to work at analysing their own problems, and which enabled us to hear the views of a cross-section of the community, not just the most vociferous and articulate.

The method basically consisted of inviting randomly selected tenants, both adults and children, to small group discussions of about eight people, and inviting the same groups back again up to three times over a couple of months. This stage was preceded by a questionnaire survey of most of the households on the estate carried out by SCPR. The main purpose of the survey was to provide a statistically firmer backcloth against which to evaluate change over a period of time. It also informed people about the scheme, and, because it was conducted by researchers calling on people in their own homes, it established vital personal contact and demonstrated that we were interested in their views. The survey was followed by leaflets delivered to every house which gave more information about the scheme and the role of the consultants, and included a form for suggestions, with a postbox address on the estate, and local contacts for enquiries.

Although it is not necessary to carry out a full-scale survey in order to encourage people to attend meetings, some kind of personal contact is essential. Other schemes based on this one which have excluded the survey have found it extraordinarily hard to get people to come to meetings, unless they were visited a number of times, and in some cases actually taken to the first meeting.

The group meetings – the core of the Cunningham Road scheme – were well attended, and almost everyone returned to subsequent meetings. Because the groups were small and met several times residents got a chance to develop and consider their views together over a period of time; to look again at the problems between meetings; and to talk to their friends and neighbours. SCPR were able to show slides of the estate to stimulate discussion; to pass ideas from one group to another; to take groups' ideas to the Council for comment or costing, and to take the Council's (or our own) ideas back to the residents for consideration. It was also possible to get senior Council officers to discuss problems with residents in these small and low-key sessions and through them to establish dialogue. Finally, SCPR were able to report back their findings from the discussions for endorsement by the group participants. These findings were then reported to the Council.[1]

From the residents' point of view the value of this method was that they all got a chance to speak (this was the reason many of them gave for bothering to come to the first meeting); they got a chance to put their views to the local authority, and get listened to; and they got a sense of being a community: it was the first time that people who did not know each other had got together and discovered they had common problems. The fact that those attending the groups saw themselves as doing a specific job (for which we paid them £1.50 a meeting[2]) provided them with neutral ground on which to meet and talk and get to know each other without feeling they had to commit themselves to anything.

The suspicion and hostility that often exist between Council and tenants, and the preconceptions that each side has of the other, do not encourage rational discussion. A neutral third party is often needed to help them to break out of that relationship. If, as in this case, an unbiased picture of the needs and priorities of tenants is sought, it is helpful if, in addition, the consultant is not identified with particular resources or responsibilities.

Two things emerged clearly from the group discussions: the low morale of the residents, who generally felt hopeless about the prospect of either making or seeing things get better; and the gap in understanding and communication between the tenants and the Council. Eighteen months later the Chief Environmental Officer wrote: 'Anyone with experience knows that there will be a communication gap, but in this case the project revealed a gap of immense scale, and not only that, but the fact that actions and the motives for those actions were totally misinterpreted. Schemes for the improvement of an area could be counter-productive if the reasons for the scheme were not fully understood by those affected by it. Similarly it was not fully understood how the community set its priorities. These priorities are often different from the priorities perceived by the authority . . . Also loud and clear came over the frustration of individuals who were unable themselves to understand the system by which society is run, and how or to whom to communicate and get results. From this frustration comes aggression, apathy and helplessness.'

The major problems described by the Cunningham Road residents were anxiety about security, dissatisfaction with the Council's performance over repairs and maintenance, and disturbance and destruction caused by young people. The young people felt they had nowhere to go and nothing to do without being harassed by adults.

Basically these problems result on the one hand from poor planning and design, and on the other from poor management. These often overlap, but an example of poor design was ill-fitting windows in the old houses, many of which either would not open, or would not close, or the glass would break if they did. This made houses highly vulnerable to thieves, and accounted for many of the broken windows round the estate. Broken windows are a recognised incitement to vandals.

The children's playgrounds on the new part of the estate were an example of both poor planning and poor design. Intended for small children, they are close to the new dwellings; but since they were the only areas on the estate which were lit and dry and had things to sit on, teenagers from the older part congregated there. They were bullying the little children, breaking the play equipment, and keeping families awake at night by banging the swings and shouting. When asked, the teenagers said they did not particularly enjoy being a nuisance or destroying things, but they had nowhere else to go, nothing better to do, and felt picked on by adults. They certainly did not seem good at thinking of constructive things to do, but this is not unusual, and therefore needs to be taken into account by planners. The teenagers' solution was to build a hut for themselves where they could do just what they wanted. Their requirements were that it should have seating, be lit, and not too far from the houses. They seemed excited by discussing what might be done to the estate and were eager to be involved in making improvements to it, such as painting murals on the graffiti-covered walkways and planting trees in public places, both of which had been suggested by the adult groups. But they needed someone to get them going.

Problems with garden fencing provided examples of both poor planning and poor management. Tenants of the old houses, with their long back gardens, have to provide their own fencing. Because of the cost of good fencing, many of the gardens were protected by iron sheeting, wire and boarding, while others were fenced so inadequately that they were overrrun by dogs and children. The front gardens had also been a hotchpotch of fencing and hedging, but before we arrived the Council, with the best intentions but without warning, had torn up the lot, replacing it with neat dwarf walls. Not surprisingly tenants felt resentful at having their hedges uprooted without consultation, particularly as the walls are completely ineffective in terms of protecting the gardens, keeping out neither children, nor dogs, nor litter.

Houses with cracked facades, broken fencing and walls on the older part of the estate

The back gardens of the new houses have excellent fencing, but tenants complained that the open-plan frontage gave them no privacy: tradesmen took shortcuts over the grass, and children played football under and against their windows. Inadequate fencing was a crucial contribution to the sense residents had of being unable to protect themselves, and of having no rights.

Resentment about the state of the older houses seemed to have been exacerbated by the new dwellings. The rents in both are almost the same, and though the new dwellings are higher density, with smaller rooms and gardens, the residents in the old houses do not see that: they see their newness, modern fittings, and good fencing; and they do not feel it is fair.

There is no doubt that tenants were far more concerned about the security and comfort of their homes, and details which aggravated them daily, than about the general look of their surroundings. Repainting the houses was a great deal more urgent, they felt, than planting trees (both of which were already planned by the Council); otherwise, as one resident exclaimed, 'The houses will laugh at the trees.' And although painting the outsides of the houses was a high priority, it was not nearly as important as maintenance and repair. People expressed the fear that painting would merely be a cosmetic job, temporarily disguising the cracks and leaks.

The general impression was that people found it such a struggle to keep their homes secure and comfortable that they had no energy or inclination to do anything about the world outside their front doors. In addition they had come to see 'authority' as the enemy, doing things *to* them, never *for* them, and tended to put an unfavourable construction on anything the authorities – particularly the Council – did.

They felt generally neglected: the police did not bother to do anything about crime on the estate, so it was seldom worth calling them when something happened; the Council dumped 'problem families' on them. They also felt frustrated by a sense of petty restriction: the Council did nothing to prevent vandalism and the disintegration of street lighting, but exercised such controls as not allowing tenants to plant hedges, or paint their own front doors. The sense of powerlessness had led to a feeling of hopelessness, of indifference in some, and hostility in others.

It was these feelings that the scheme was able to do something about. Previously there had been no special organisation on the estate, no way in which people who did not already know each other could meet and talk; tenants had always communicated individually with the Council and usually only when they were frustrated and angry; the Council had only communicated with tenants through short official notices. Through the small group meetings people on the estate got to know each other and share problems. They also were able to meet local authority officers in a constructive atmosphere – in which both sides were amazed by the reasonableness of the other. The meetings provided a forum in which people began to see themselves as a community and to realise that together they did have power, and could influence what happened on the estate.

A number of things happened immediately. The tenants who had come to the group meetings, excited by this sense of community power, called a public meeting at which they set up a Residents' Association. The association set about organising street parties and outings for children and bullying the Council about repairs. An adventure playground, which was under construction before the scheme began, opened near the estate: a playleader was appointed who involved mothers with playground activities and organised children to plant trees and start a mural on one of the walkways. The Council responded instantly to some of the complaints and suggestions, allowing tenants to choose colours for their houses and encouraging them to plant hedges and put fencing on top of the dwarf walls; pavements and street lighting were repaired, and some outstanding house repairs were dealt with. At the request of tenants a beat policeman was assigned to the estate.

It is now over two years since the scheme began, and although the effects have not been evaluated at the time of writing, it is possible to make a number of observations about what has been happening on the estate. The Residents' Association is thriving, despite occasional internal difficulties, and over two-thirds of the estate are fully paid up members. It has regular monthly meetings with Council officers over repairs, and the repairs and maintenance situation now seems to be satisfactory both to tenants and Council.[3]

The adventure playground has only begun to live up to expectations 18 months after opening: within weeks of its opening it was so severely vandalised that the Council closed it down. The original damage was said to have been done by teenagers from another estate, but may well have been completed by the children for whom it was designed. Since then it has been intermittently open and closed, and there has been a high turnover of playleaders. At last there is a playleader who seems likely to stay, and the adventure playground is well used. There has been no more trouble on the playgrounds in the new part of the estate.

A long-planned Youth and Community Centre has opened nearby, quite independently of the scheme. This may have contributed to the general sense of improvement. But so far the community side had not been extensively used by people from the estate although the youth side is popular with the children.

The impression from talking to members of the Residents' Association, Council officers, representatives of other agencies, and based on our own observation, is that the estate is a better place to live.

There seems no doubt that there is less vandalism: there is little visible sign of litter, broken glass or other breakage; such graffiti as there are were there before the scheme started; despite everyone's fears, almost all the trees planted two years ago are still standing; a house remained empty for six months, unboarded and unprotected, and yet undamaged, which residents tell us would have been unthinkable two years ago. In addition, residents say that teenagers are seldom a nuisance; the beat policeman reports a 'dramatic decrease in crime', and some quietening of the few families who had been terrorising the neighbourhood.

There is generally a feeling of more confidence on the estate, and no longer a sense of being under perpetual siege. Residents and authorities say it looks a different place; many tenants are doing up their front gardens, encouraged, they say, by the brightly painted houses. People now know their neighbours, and feel that the estate really is becoming a community. The increased confidence of tenants in dealing with problems is particularly noticeable; they know whom to go to in the Council to get specific results; due to the beat bobby, they now trust the police to handle situations sensitively, and therefore often discuss problems with them before crises can develop. Two years ago when teenagers were causing a disturbance or smashing things, nobody dared to go out and tell them to stop. Now, residents tell us, they seldom hesitate, partly because they know the teenagers individually, and, more importantly, because they know they can rely on their neighbours to come out and support them.

Trees were planted on the estate when the improvement scheme was under way

DESIGN COUNCIL

Well kept gardens are symptoms of the increased confidence of residents in the estate which developed as the scheme took effect

Although the picture is generally very encouraging, problems are not completely solved. Vandalism and crime have not disappeared, although they seem to have decreased. There are some curious discrepancies: for instance, residents and police say that there is much less crime, yet this is not reflected in police statistics. The police assume this is accounted for by increased reporting by people on the estate. Again, residents are pleased that street lighting is seldom out of order; yet Council records show that more repairs are being done to street lighting on the estate than two years ago. At the moment it is difficult to be sure whether the explanation is increased frequency of repair, or more vandalism, or both. The Council think it is the former. Although working relations with the Council are now vastly improved, communications about plans and policies still leave room for misconceptions. An exchange about traffic schemes was recently conducted by letter, and it became clear that the parties had completely misunderstood each other. An attempt by the Council to do what residents wanted could easily have backfired and been resented as dictatorial and uncaring Council action. The Residents' Association has established itself successfully, but still has some difficulty over organisation, managing its aspirations, and communicating clearly with its own membership.

What has happened to bring about the positive changes on the estate? The normal approach to 'problem' estates is to provide things: to spend money. Very little money has been spent on Cunningham Road that was not already allocated to the area, although some was transferred from other budgets so that small repairs could be done quickly. However, Council officers have given a good deal of time to the tenants, which has enabled them to establish a new relationship, and it is this relationship which has raised the tenants' morale. Council officers are beginning to treat tenants as individuals to whom explanations are due, and who should be consulted about plans which will affect them and their environment. As a result, tenants feel they are of consequence; they feel they are involved in decision making; and this has led to their beginning to feel a personal responsibility for what goes on. The Residents' Association now sees itself as responsible for organising activities for the young, for raising money for playing fields, for making sure the Council get repairs done and that the police protect vulnerable households. For most of the tenants their relationships with the police, too, have changed. Through personal contact with the beat bobby, they have come to trust the police, and the police have a different attitude towards them. They now work together to keep down crime, and to some extent also residents are beginning to police themselves.

Given the hostile situation two years ago, none of this could have come about without some sort of catalyst, leading to positive results which people could actually see. The way in which this scheme brought people together allowed them to believe that change might be possible, that things could get better.

This could not have happened if the Council had not committed themselves to the scheme, had not responded to tenants' problems and suggestions, and continued to respond. Eighteen months after the scheme began the Chief Executive (of the Council) wrote: 'This particular experience has uplifted an area of extremely poor morale. Rising expectations bring rising demands. This particular experiment is forcing a number of conclusions upon the Council:

'It reveals the difficulty of presenting a corporate or co-ordinated approach . . . it reveals in sharp relief the fragmented and unco-ordinated nature of public services.

'It forces communication not only between the Council and the residents, but between the Council and the other institutions . . .

'An exercise such as this requires a considerable investment of manpower from a senior level.

'. . . It throws into sharp relief the isolation of the Council . . . The major conclusion must be that what began as an exercise to learn more about vandalism has now become an exercise in direct involvement in the daily life of a particularly troubled community.

'Vandalism is one expression of the frustrations and disappointments of that community.'

'Our present conclusion', he now says, 'is that many of the traditional anti-vandalism campaign methods are aiming at the wrong target. The best way forward for a local authority to tackle vandalism is firstly to listen and then to understand, and then to respond. Even to do this an authority has to change its traditional position and behaviour.'[3]

What started as an anti-vandalism project, and seems successful as such, has in the long run had implications far wider than its original terms of reference. It has underlined, among other things: the possibility of improving the lot of council tenants without necessarily massive capital spending; the importance, and difficulty, of dialogue between residents and the Council; the importance of estate morale, and the ways in which this is affected by communications between tenants and Council; and the latent possibilities for self-help among tenants themselves.

Largely as a result of this experience, Halton Council has now adopted a package of changes which emphasise the importance of improving estate management. These changes include a switch of personnel from professionals whose jobs assumed continual capital expenditure into jobs which are face to face with the public; a reorganisation of the housing department on an 'area officer' basis, increasing both the number and status of people in that department (made possible by the preceding switch). The relationship of the housing department to the building department has become one of client and supplier and, among other things, changes in documentation and administration are being made to make area-based programmes manageable and assessable. Also, operational training programmes have been set up for those in face-to-face contact with the public.

Changes such as these may have many different kinds of effect, but they are all to some degree related to a linked set of objectives: to improve the delivery of services to residents; to improve communications, understanding and relations between Council and residents; and to increase residents' satisfaction with housing conditions and services.

This may seem a far cry from the original objective of cutting down vandalism, but if one accepts vandalism as 'one expression of the frustrations and disappointments of a community' perhaps it is only through such radical measures that a long-lasting effect on vandalism can be achieved. It is not easy, but it seems to work, and Halton Council is acting upon it. To quote Halton's Head of Housing Services:

It is in the nature of bureaucracy to crunch everything into a shape or form with which it is used to dealing. Consequently bureaucracy has difficulty in dealing with the input from residents which very often won't conform to the norm. At best it is like sand in the well oiled works, at worst it can give the system acute indigestion. It is axiomatic that systems are developed for the benefit of the authority and its officers but not necessarily for the tenant. One of the results of the project has been to make us look carefully at our systems from the client's point of view so that response is more sympathetic to the client, even if this had to be achieved at the expense of traditional management practices.

Lessons learned from the project have led to changes in the structure of the housing organisation and these lessons are now being implemented throughout the Council's housing policy and practice. Both tenants and authority are finding the process rather painful – but in the end I am convinced that the exercise is not only worth while, but necessary.

Notes

[1] *Community Planning Project: Cunningham Road Improvement Scheme – Interim Report:* Alan Hedges and James Spence, SCPR. Available from Barry Rose (Publishers) Ltd, Little London, Chichester, Sussex PO19 1PG. Price £2.25, plus 35p postage and packing.

[2] Eight people (out of the 60 paid) asked that their fee be given to the Council to be put towards the adventure playground.

[3] Two years ago (October 1976) the average delay on routine repairs throughout Halton Housing was nearly three months. The Council reckoned the delay on repairs for the Cunningham Road Estate was probably five months. At the time of writing the average delay in Halton is still nearly three months, but the Housing Manager considers that the Cunningham Road Estate 'could be getting a wee bit of preferential treatment'.

Vandalism in housing estates: where it occurs and how it can be prevented

by David White, *New Society*

The architect, it has been suggested, suffers from role inflation: too much is expected of him. When things go wrong, too often he is used as a whipping-boy. An over-zealous interpretation of architectural determinism – the theory that the built environment affects behaviour – blames architects for vandalism, which is seen as a reaction to unsympathetic surroundings. The architect of local authority housing particularly has to live with what he has built in a way that the architect of private housing does not. He is holding its hand long after private housing schemes have learnt to walk on their own. And so the responsibility for the failures of materials in use and for the more fundamental 'errors' of building form – both supposed triggers of vandalism – remains with the architect.

To an extent, it is right that this should happen. The provision of mass public housing has meant a distancing of designer and user. It is salutary for the planner and architect to be shown that the way in which a housing estate is used is often different from the way expected.

The possible changes in use of housing estates over a period of time are quite as important a design factor as the cost-in-use of the materials used to build them. In this respect, vandalism and the abuse of housing estates (which can express a change in use of an estate) are negative but direct responses to the architect's original intentions.

However, sociologists, architects and planners are recognising that the built environment is merely one of the factors which influence the way in which people use or abuse their surroundings. It cannot be considered in isolation. Just as there are no absolute offenders in building types (David Canter, an environmental psychologist at Surrey University, has put forward a cogent defence of high-rise buildings) so there is no panacea in building design. Nor, necessarily, will an improvement and strengthening of fixtures and fittings provide an answer to vandalism *by itself*.

Alison Ravetz of Leeds University, noting the abuse of a well designed playground and a well fitted public lavatory, both newly installed on a Leeds housing estate, points out that 'it is a natural reaction of designers to dismiss all failures as the result of past errors, with the implications that these could not be repeated . . '. it evades the fact that the same categories of use, and consequently the same failures, arise in quite new environments, despite their physical differences.'[1]

Should the architect or planner simply ignore vandalism, saying that there is nothing that he, individually, can do? This might be justified were not design and management closely linked, and the efforts of architects, housing managers, maintenance officers and tenants interdependent. Ease of maintenance will depend on the use of sturdy or easily replaceable materials. Sound surveillance of housing estates by a caretaker or, more importantly, the tenants themselves, will depend on the design of layouts which can be policed. Allocations will depend on types of building (high-rise, for example, will be less suitable for families with young children) and the provision and siting of play space. The designer is involved at every stage, though the actual physical design may be only part of the 'package'. Designing against vandalism, therefore, encompasses everything from the manufacture of stout door hinges to the management, and self-management, of people.

The local authority's approach to the design of its housing will be both diagnostic and prognostic. On the level of materials and fittings, it must look back, find out what has been damaged and replace it with something stronger. This is basic self-defence, reactive, even negative in approach. It must also look forward and avoid or allow for future damage by building in easy-to-maintain or replaceable materials and fittings. This is good husbandry, and positive in approach. But it will succeed only if it is linked to a system of management which constantly responds to feedback from users and maintenance (see page 54).

For local authorities who feel that they do themselves have the resources for this kind of analysis there is a growing corpus of casework to draw on. The Building Research Establishment produced a *vade mecum* for architects of housing estates in 1971. It was drawn up on the assumption that architects who discovered that their handiwork was being mistreated would want to do something about it.

Working from local authority repair notes, the BRE summary (*Wilful Damage on Housing Estates*, Digest 132) found that the most frequently reported damage was to glass: at foot level, and in entrances and access ways, particularly in buildings which housed a number of children. It also pointed out that damaged glazing, more than any other single feature, contributes to the vandalised look of a building.

In the long term such damage suggests that preventive rather than defensive measures are needed: modifications to the design and layout of housing estates, caretakers to provide supervision and a housing allocation policy which distributes families with children more equably. But, with the immediate needs of the user in mind, the BRE summary confines itself to commonsense precautions and indicates finishes, materials and design features that work. Collating and analysing its own housing repair notes, and devising from them a preventive

A broken window in a passage opening on to deck access in a block of flats

design guide for architects, is the first step a local authority should take.

It may be thought that only the largest authorities have experienced a sufficient range of damage and have the resources and the incentive to do this. However many authorities are now forming building consortia to share the economies of scale of method building where designs are standardised and professional services shared. Within these consortia, a standard approach to damage to public buildings is a necessary and logical step.

The Consortium for Method Building, a grouping of seven local authorities, including Somerset and Berkshire counties, estimates that vandalism and unnecessary damage to county buildings costs the members around £200,000 a year. It has found, as might be expected, that the most serious damage, involving the highest cost in replacement, is to glazing, lavatories, doors and general fixtures and fittings.

In response, the consortium's architects have drawn up a checklist of likely damage and the remedies or precautions that should be taken to avoid it (which we reproduce on page 95). The key instruction, in almost all areas, is to aim at robust construction.

Much of the advice is directed specifically at the design of school buildings: for example, precautions to be taken fitting out sanitary installations, a prime target for schoolchildren. Account is also taken of who will occupy buildings: for example, although, generally, knobs should be used rather than lever handles (which can be ripped off) an exception should be made for old people's homes: old people find knobs difficult to operate and the problem of rough treatment does not arise. Overall, however, the checklist applies to all building types, method-built or not.

The consortium's working party felt that the likelihood of vandalism occurring was affected, broadly, by two things: first, the general building design — its siting, the relationship and adequacy of play space and circulation spaces, its robustness in areas of high use and risk of attack, the relationship of its parts and the overall atmosphere created; and secondly, detail design and the choice of materials and fittings.

To give guidance to project architects in the future, the working party plans to investigate the influence of building design on the incidence and extent of vandalism, and to incorporate design advice either in the consortium design guide or in office materials.

The working party also intends to produce standard details and layouts for areas particularly liable to attack, and to select ranges of fixtures and fittings with known good performance and robustness. The more general appraisal of building design has yet to begin, but the checklist is a start at the more detailed level of self-defence.

Local authorities' investigations of vandalism have revealed the need to differentiate between 'actual' and 'supposed' vandalism. Not all damage is deliberate, wanton or without motive. In many cases, it can be blamed on weak detailing, poor workmanship, inadequate maintenance, misuse or general neglect. This is underlined in a survey of housing schemes carried out by the Greater London Council. Although the worst cases of vandalism are normally found in high-rise estates, this survey concentrated on low-rise, high-density housing built in the last decade.

The inventory of damage it revealed is predictable, and mirrors the experience of other local authorities. There is a consistent pattern in what gets hit, with similar items being repeatedly attacked. Glazing is always a temptation to the vandal, particularly in circulation areas, drying rooms, and other communal areas. Light fittings are constantly vandalised. Plastics rainwater pipes and guttering, offering a leg up to flat roofs, rarely survive.

Often these features *are* wantonly damaged – glazing is frequently attacked even before the housing is handed over to the client – but just as often they are the victims of escalating abuse and neglect triggered off by accidental damage. Light fittings which are left loosely secured during installation or after servicing provoke vandalism. Neglect is infectious, and accidental damage which is left unrepaired encourages further damage. Areas of 'low esteem' are particularly vulnerable. Anything temporary, slipshod, or over-used, anything indeed which suggests that the housing authority is indifferent to the well-being of its tenants will invite casual ill-treatment.

The need for strong, sensible materials and detailing is therefore clear. The intention is not primarily to reinforce buildings against the efforts of the determined vandal – hardcore vandalism is committed by only a small though persistent minority, and budgets prohibit the most extreme precautions against it. Architects may argue that the cost-in-use of initially more expensive materials works out cheaper in the long run. However, the present system of financing public housing works against any broad application of this principle. Expenditure for capital schemes is kept quite separate from expenditure on running costs, and it is not possible to ask for a larger capital expenditure on the grounds that running costs will be proportionately reduced.

The real need is to reduce the *excuses* for casual vandalism. Building failures, the GLC have found, are the commonest triggers of vandalism. Tough detailing is needed, for example, to prevent damage to the coping ends and exposed edges of brick walls. Otherwise a minor initial failure can encourage a major collapse. When doors fail in public areas (communal entrances, garages and refuse chambers) they positively invite vandalism. The GLC suggests the use of stronger ironmongery.

The evidence that initial accidental damage triggers further deliberate damage argues the case for more attention to detailing. It also, however, suggests there are more fundamental errors in building layout which could be avoided at the design stage.

Lighting at ground level is highly vulnerable. On one side of this ramp the lights are clumsily protected by wire grilles (shown). On the other side of the ramp the lighting units have been removed altogether. It would have been better if the design of the ramp had not required this location of the lights, but since it did, vandal-proof versions designed with polycarbonate glazing should have been used

Damage occurs most frequently where there is little or no surveillance: for example, in garages, refuse chambers and lifts. Damage also occurs in areas where ownership is ambiguous, the no-man's-land for which no one in particular feels responsible: for example, deck access to flats where the aim is to reproduce a street in the air. To this extent, certain building and estate layouts can be said to encourage vandalism.

This idea has been most fully developed by Oscar Newman, who has termed such no-man's-land 'indefensible space'. Newman has suggested that the amount of vandalism a building suffers is related directly to the amount of 'indefensible space' it has. The assumption that this is the major factor determining vandalism has been attacked. Newman's theory ignores tenure, architects argue. Ownership may be quite as important as territory. A survey by Sheena Wilson, while at the Home Office Research Unit, to test Newman's theory gave only limited support.[2]

Her examination of 52 housing estates in two London boroughs suggests that the design of buildings does not affect overall levels of vandalism. Tower blocks, in particular, are no more susceptible to vandalism than other types of building.

However, her survey *does* suggest that different types of building encourage different types of vandalism. Sheena Wilson found that in large buildings where access routes were very public and people could come and go unchallenged, communal areas were heavily vandalised. In tower blocks, damage was concentrated round entrance ways, which again were public enough to act as through routes for all and sundry. One design solution, Sheena Wilson suggests, is to make entrances less inviting to outsiders, and thereby build a sense of privacy for insiders. An extreme solution, which Ealing Borough has chosen, is the installation of Entryphones at the base of tower blocks.

The use and over-use of access routes are critical factors which are closely linked to the amounts of damage that different buildings sustain. In an examination of 18 housing estates in Lambeth for the Lambeth Inner Area Study,[3] a team from the Shankland Cox partnership suggests that staircase access blocks, in which a single entry has a door and leads to about 12 dwellings, suffer the least damage. The worst instances of vandalism occur on heavily used access ways – often used as a through route by outsiders.

This deck access passageway to flats in a high-rise block is remarkably damage free, since it is a perfect example of 'indefensible space': it does not appear to belong to anyone in particular; strangers would not be challenged; and it offers enough privacy for the vandal to operate undetected

The most vulnerable access ways are those which link the flats in deck access and continuous gallery type buildings. These thoroughfares are in general use (in a deck access building 200 dwellings may be accessible from one entry point) yet are the responsibility of no one in particular. Here, the *type* of building is undeniably responsible, for whole tracts of 'indefensible space'.

Buildings of this scale produce other problems, which make natural policing by tenants even less likely. As the Lambeth study points out, stringent fire regulations tend to produce labyrinthine entrances, dark or full of glazed screens, which are themselves an additional target. The study feels that the single, protected staircase is to be preferred to the earlier idea of alternative escape routes, since it is a less anonymous form of access. It also limits the number of dwellings using it to comply with fire regulations.

The lesson is that entrances and staircases which are isolated and out of sight of the residents become, as the GLC architects' department says 'vandal temptation zones'. It points out that fire precaution requirements which call for the separation of primary staircases from flats and maisonettes (either by fire restricting doors to enclosed staircases or by individual lobbies with extra outer doors to individual flats) create precisely these zones.

Obviously fire precautions cannot be brushed aside. But if, the GLC suggests, each staircase serves fewer dwellings, this will reduce the *scale* of the building and an approaching intruder will be easily identified. If six people share the same staircase, each one will know the other five. If sixty share a staircase, this kind of natural surveillance is impossible. Above a certain number (about ten), tenants are no *more* aware of their immediate neighbours than of neighbours in distant parts of the building.

In the same way, although entrance halls which are used for short cuts can be sealed off, the necessity for this could have been avoided altogether: housing planned in cul-de-sac arrangements with entrances used by known residents (that is, known to each other) seldom suffers from vandalism.

Surveillance is the key to any successful new design, and a building that reduces surveillance encourages vandalism. This idea has been developed by Roy Worskett, Bath City Architect. He argues that redevelopment schemes which take people from established neighbourhoods and isolate them from one another in tower blocks, break down any sense of community. What is also lost, he emphasises, is the self-policing of a community.

The mix of different uses in the older urban areas, Worskett argues, does an important job preserving a safe and successful environment, because it makes surveillance easier and provides a focus for neighbourhood interaction. In other words, buildings that have been developed on a human scale, buildings which directly reflect the needs of the people for whom they were built and of the people who are living in them today, are more 'sociable', and therefore discourage anti-social behaviour.

In cities like his own, therefore, Worskett argues that rehabilitation and sensitive infill are vastly preferable to comprehensive redevelopment. For the architect who has to provide local authority housing of considerable size, the lessons of scale still apply, and the aim should be to keep scale small. An estate can be very large, but consist of spaces which are intimate in scale. The Lambeth study attempted to measure scale in terms of the number of dwellings which can be seen from a typical vantage point. It then set the scales of different estates against the estates' relative popularity. This showed that where scale is small and an estate breaks down easily into small units, there is a greater sense of identification between the tenants and their own unit of the estate. Where the unit is large – over 100 dwellings visible from a typical vantage point – a sense of identity is lost.

Scale does seem to have an important bearing on the amount of vandalism estates suffer. The Lambeth study found that a factor common to all estates where vandalism is least apparent is small-scale, well-maintained green spaces where the common areas appear to belong to the residents rather than everyone and no one.

On the other hand, open spaces which are severed by short cuts appeared to the Lambeth study team to be heavily vandalised. Problems occur particularly where private space (which 'belongs') comes up sharply against public space (which does not appear to belong). Ground-floor dwellings in old blocks are often exposed to passers-by, particularly where the open space outside is unprotected. Fenced private gardens, providing a *cordon sanitaire*, can improve this situation.

One of these ground-floor flats is protected by a wall and a gate, but the fate of the flat next door with its boarded window and accumulated rubbish shows the defensive use of a clearly defined private zone

Generally, the Lambeth study team felt the need for dividing the space round buildings into three clearly divided zones: a private zone, maybe gardens, around the dwelling itself; a semi-private zone, maybe a courtyard, shared by 20 to 50 dwellings, so that intruders are noticed; and a public zone beyond that, shared by the area as a whole.

The design of buildings and the layout of housing estates therefore has at least to take account of territory, and show clearly which space belongs to whom. This is particularly important where there are concentrations of children, for experience on housing estates shows that the 'dead ground' of unsupervised garages, lifts and access ways is the favourite playground of children. Sheena Wilson's survey of London estates shows quite clearly that child density is a critical factor determining degrees of vandalism. She found that all types of building were likely to experience some problems of vandalism once the ratio of school-age children went above five to every ten dwellings, or where the overall number of children in a block exceeded 20.

This vandal-proof milk float operates on a north London housing estate with a high child population. Not only is the milk securely locked up while the milkman is making deliveries inside the flats, but it is packed in cardboard cartons since milk bottles had proved a popular missile

Child densities are the responsibility of the local authority, who will handle allocations, rather than the architect. Yet certain building types will exacerbate child density problems. High-rise blocks which house large numbers of children are particularly susceptible to vandalism. The Department of the Environment design bulletin *Children at Play* recommends that local authorities should house families with children on or near the ground.

The designer can also be involved in attempts to canalise children's play. The simple provision of play space is not necessarily the answer. In her survey of a Leeds housing estate, Alison Ravetz found that a new playground quickly became a target for vandalism. Often what is needed is a clear definition of what space is *not* to be used for. The sense of ownership and the opportunities for surveillance, which the right scale gives, can help. A Shankland Cox team, in a study of private housing,[4] discovered that adults resent the play of children *they do not know* far more than that of children who live nearby. A number of smaller, more localised play spaces, clearly defined as such, therefore might avoid conflicts. Alternatively, the Lambeth study suggests that play areas might be moved around from one part of the estate to another like a form of crop rotation: this not only gives the grass a chance to grow, but also means the nuisance of living near a large playground is shared.

The key to both broad and detailed design attempts to discourage vandalism and encourage sociable living, however, is management. Not simply the management of 'us' (the tenants) by 'them' (the local authority housing department) but the interdependent efforts of planners, project architects, housing departments, maintenance departments, caretakers and tenants. Vandalism tends to be seen as a practice isolated from normal behaviour, and therefore solutions are expected to be simple and dramatic. In fact, most vandalism belongs within the category of wear and tear, and solutions are more likely to be found in the mundane day-to-day maintenance of buildings. Instead of throwing up novel solutions to a novel problem, the study of vandalism suggests a comprehensive mix of known remedies, none of which will do the trick on its own. It also suggests implicitly that local authorities look carefully at how they manage their buildings, and, more particularly, at the relationship between themselves and their tenants.

Notes

[1] Ravetz, A: 'The uses and abuses of the planned environment', *RIBA Journal*, April 1972
[2] Wilson, S: DoE summary paper
[3] Shankland Cox and Associates: *Private Housing in London: people and environment in three Wates Housing Schemes*, 1969
[4] *Ibid*

Feedback:
how local authorities can learn from their experience of vandalism

by David White, *New Society*

'The architect has so little freedom to manoeuvre that he doesn't always allow for vandalism in his designs. And there is a tendency for him to design a building the way he thinks *he's* going to use it' (local authority architect). A common criticism of local authority buildings is that the architects who design them never meet the people who will actually use them. The implied suggestion is that, if they did, fundamental mistakes in design could be avoided. This is perhaps a naive view. However, the architect who visits his housing estate or school a year after its completion will appreciate, from the evidence of under-use, over-use and abuse, that there is often a serious mismatching of the designer's intentions and the users' behaviour. Vandalism is the clearest though most perplexing evidence of this mismatch.

An architect, moving on to other jobs, cannot be expected to monitor the progress of all his buildings (though school buildings are so monitored). If he is able to draw on the accumulated experiences of other schemes, monitored by maintenance departments, he will, at the design stage, be able to allow for and avoid likely abuses.

This, broadly, is a feedback system. It can take the form of an information bank or a forum, but it will depend on up-the-line reports and the free exchange of information. Ideally, specific measures of self-defence against vandalism, such as the installation of tougher ironmongery, need the back-up of such a system to monitor performance and update recommendations.

A model for the way in which a full feedback system works is provided by the education branch of the GLC architects' department. Here, the architect is *obliged* to seek expert advice on maintenance, security, and fire prevention at the time he is working on the element of the building. In this way he can, at an early stage balance the conflicting demands of, say, security and fire safety: the general requirement for secure windows may have to be modified to provide access for the fire brigade for fire fighting or rescue services.

Certain information is crucial at the early design stage. The security officer and local police have to be consulted to assess the type of neighbourhood in which the school will be built, and the degree of security needed for the building.

The key relationship, however, is between the job architect and the regional maintenance officer (RMO). The RMO is at the centre of the feedback system, and is responsible for the building reports on which it is based. A job architect must consult the RMO throughout the preparation of his scheme. Even when the scheme is handed over, he may be asked to do additional preventive work.

The maintenance officer collates a *curriculum vitae* of the building both from the architect's report, which records the use of any special materials, and from the design team's progress report, which provides a construction history and details of any changes in the client's brief. Six months after handover, the clerk of works, job architect and RMO complete a defects report. At this stage, buildings can become especially vulnerable to casual vandalism. If neither the architect nor the contractor admits liability for faults, these can remain uncorrected; and defects which are not quickly put right encourage progressive damage. In the GLC system, however, the maintenance officer can take over when this happens and authorise repairs until liability is settled.

Even then, the architect cannot wash his hands of the building. A year later, when the building is in use, a similar review takes place, and two to three years after handover the architect and a maintenance representative appraise the building. This is, the GLC say, a dispassionate business. There are no recriminations. The architect is shown what has gone wrong, and, more rewardingly, what has worked well.

Thereafter, maintenance keeps a regular eye on the building. The users of the building, parents and teachers, feed back their experience through the education officer. Primary school heads and teachers also answer technical appraisal questionnaires.

Feedback is sifted to provide the kind of detailed design guidance given in the section on schools, which concentrates on the detailing of fixtures and fittings which are most severely and frequently damaged (windows, doors and lavatories). A security design guide has been produced. Its lessons are also incorporated in a *Building Users Guide*, a maintenance manual for school caretakers.

Such a system is, in the long term, well equipped to deal with occupational damage and vandalism because it puts maintenance at the centre of operations; collating building-in-use information and feeding back its lessons to job architects.

Could such a system be used for the building and maintenance of housing estates? There are substantial differences between the administration of housing and education which would modify features of the system. Housing yardsticks, for example, restrict expenditure whereas education is allocated a lump sum. Housing architects cannot afford to raise standards to avoid maintenance or vandalism problems in the way that education architects can. For the same reason modification to, say, door hinges has to be taken at a slower pace by housing architects. The money is not available.

The general principle, however, is sound. Local authorities are recognising that to protect schools from vandalism, architect, education department and security expert (usually the police) have to liaise and exchange information. In its efforts to tackle vandalism in its schools, Bedfordshire County Council has decided to report all incidents to the police. In turn the police have agreed to feed the information, and estimated costs, into the police computer for a monthly vandalism return.

The county's working party on vandalism suggested that an examination of these returns by crime prevention officers and the county education department would show how the various school buildings are being attacked, and that this information should be passed on to architects involved in designing new schools.

Systems of feedback, major or modest, are admirable as far as they go. If, however (as architects themselves complain), recommendations from architects' feedback are ignored further down the line, or if feedback stops short at maintenance (taking little account of the *actual* needs of users), these systems do not go far enough. The study of Lambeth housing estates carried out by Shankland Cox[1] revealed wide gaps between the tenants and the maintenance and housing departments.

A common complaint on housing estates is that damage is left unrepaired for too long (and unrepaired damage triggers off further damage). In her survey[2] of an outlying estate in Leeds Alison Ravetz found that the estate office blamed tenants for failing to repair damage. In fact, records showed that since 1960 more than 3000 house improvements had been sanctioned by the authority and carried out at the tenants' own expense.

A lack of communication between tenants and housing department means that there is little attempt to find what people want *now* (as opposed to when the estate was designed), and therefore no assessment of where and how the use of the estate has changed.

A survey of Lambeth housing estates as part of an Inner Areas Study[3] revealed incidentally the same pattern; good features that had failed were not removed, but left as they were. In one case, children's swings had been chained up for years rather than weeks. Unlovely features of the estate which were misused were not removed but crudely repaired.

The signs of under-use, over-use or abuse of a housing estate, Alison Ravetz suggests,[4] are clues that the present use of the estate is different from the use originally intended by the designer. Measures which do not recognise change of use, which merely strengthen or renew vandalised areas, are therefore unlikely to succeed on their own.

Technical feedback between maintenance office and architects' department may therefore deal with the symptoms rather than the causes of the abuse. Alison Ravetz's 'use analysis' approaches housing estates as living organisms rather than a collection of access ways and circulation areas. It treats change as the only constant factor instead of – as architects' departments tend to do – rationalising the results of change: for example paving unofficial short cuts across grassed areas, thereby regularising a spontaneous pattern of behaviour. Ravetz's analysis suggests that housing estate design that does not take account of this change will be incompatible with the habits, needs and wishes of the estate dwellers. Vandalism is the surest sign of incompatibility.

The user therefore is an unwitting provider of a negative kind of feedback. Alison Ravetz concludes that 'instead of needing more and more sophisticated designs to achieve tighter and tighter control over their effects, the designer could regard himself as only one agent among others providing built environment. Though his role is indispensable, improvements in levels of use do not devolve on him alone, but might more properly be the concern of users and managers.'[5]

'From the design point of view, you have to ask how is the building going to be managed, then design it so it's possible to manage it, then manage it properly.'[6] Oliver Cox of Shankland Cox and Partners is convinced that efficient and *responsive* management of estates (through caretaking and maintenance services) rather than design, determines the quality of the environment. In their study of Lambeth housing estates, the Shankland Cox team found that the resident caretaker is a key figure, not least as a vital mediator between tenants and maintenance department. Wherever caretakers were absent, levels of maintenance were lower, and levels of vandalism were higher. Without the link of an on-the-spot caretaker, the gap between designed, intended use and actual use (or abuse) widens. The solution, Oliver Cox suggests, is to have on hand someone who can put right minor damage at once, yet be able to rely on the back-up of the maintenance office for more extensive repairs. This resident 'handyman', Cox suggests, could be a tenant himself, who is paid for his services. However tenants and tenants' associations are perhaps justifiably suspicious of tackling larger problems of maintenance which are properly the business of the maintenance department. The majority want efficient management rather than self-management, and would like to feel that though they can more speedily put right damage themselves (because, unlike maintenance, they are on the spot) they could if necessary call in the maintenance department.

Feedback cannot be really comprehensive without some input from the users. Sheena Wilson suggests that there is a need for systematic feedback to the housing authority on the residents' satisfaction with their homes.[7] The GLC architects are carrying out an elaborate social survey to discover how people feel about their homes. The aim is to build up a file of features which people positively like and positively dislike. When the results are read off they will be fed into the architects' brief, and will determine, for example, a building's layout.

Feedback from tenants, however, appears to be largely ignored by housing departments. There is often a feeling of mutual mistrust between tenant and council, and misconceptions are common. A survey of a Widnes council estate by NACRO (see p 30) revealed that even the best intentioned efforts at improving the neighbourhood can be misinterpreted by the people they are intended to benefit, if communications between the authority and the residents are poor. Tenants are inclined to believe they are not allowed to do anything, and in some cases they think they are forbidden to do things the Council would actually *like* them to do; for example, to plant hedges in their gardens.

At this low point of relations it is impossible for the housing department to get any useful answer to the question, 'what needs to be done in the area?' The NACRO study avoided this problem by asking the question itself, analysing the answers and recommending to the Council ways in which the money could be used to help. Subsequently, both people's attitude to the Council and the actual situation on the estate were monitored for improvement.

The tenants' solution to the estate's appearance included painting the outsides of houses using a choice of colours, tree planting and road closure. There was no evidence, however, that tenants were any less likely than the local authority to be wrong or unlucky in their choices. However, the consultation stage succeeded, and showed that tenants could themselves contribute positive ideas about improving their neighbourhood, and suggest specific steps that could be taken.

Notes

[1] Shankland Cox and Associates: *Private Housing in London: people and environment in three Wates Housing Schemes*, 1969

[2] Ravetz, A: 'The uses and abuses of the planned environment', *RIBA Journal*, April 1972

[3] Lambeth Inner Area Study: *Housing Management and Design*, DoE (London, 1977)

[4] Ravetz, A, *op cit*

[5] *Ibid*

[6] Shankland Cox and Associates, *op cit*

[7] Wilson, S: DoE summary paper

Vandalism and theft in schools: how local authorities can defend themselves

by David White, *New Society*

Vandalism is a crime, or quasi-crime, of the young. Schools therefore can be expected to provide a focus for wilful damage. Local authority repair bills confirm that schools bear the brunt of vandals' attacks. In a typical industrial city with a population of over 500,000, an authority will deal with 4,000 cases of vandalism a year, of which 2,500 occur in schools. Of its total bill of £150,000, £61,000 is accounted for by damage to schools, against £44,000 for damage to housing.

The scale of the problem obviously varies with the size and nature of the local authority area. The education authority of the Greater London Council, which runs the schools within the densely populated inner London boroughs, faces an annual bill of around £1 million – enough to pay for 20 new nursery schools – for 'occupational damage'. Bedfordshire County Council, on the other hand, has calculated that over a four-month period vandalism and theft in its schools cost around £21,000. No incident cost over £1,000, so Bedfordshire was comfortably clear of the £3,000 threshold set by the Department of Education in its national survey of vandalism in schools.

Yet analyses by both authorities of what gets hit, where and how often, suggest that there are certain basic steps that all authorities can take to defend themselves and to reduce occupational damage.

The first step is to identify the damage. A survey of 15 representative local authorities by the Home Office Standing Committee on Crime Prevention, asking them to estimate the overall and specific costs of vandalism, revealed considerable imprecision. Some authorities found it difficult to distinguish between deliberate and accidental damage; the effects, after all, are the same. Damage that was deliberate but minor was often put right in the course of general maintenance, and could not be disentangled from repair and maintenance statistics.

This is perhaps no more than a reflection of imprecision on a national level. The Home Office records only incidents of malicious damage costing over £20 and many cases of vandalism cost less than this. A cut-off point is necessarily arbitrary.

In an attempt to pin down the problem with more precision, Bedfordshire asked each of its schools to complete vandalism report forms over an initial four-month survey period in 1975 and return them to the education department for analysis. The analysis first categorised the reported incidents. Vandalism was seen as a spectrum which moved from simple vandalism through vandalism coupled with theft to theft (hard crime). The majority of the 216 incidents reported were at the lower end, but about a third included theft, of which 13 per cent were coupled with vandalism.

At the other end of the spectrum, simple vandalism shades into occupational damage where, though the effect may be the same, the motive is different. Because the county's working party considered the link between vandalism and theft to be more significant than that between vandalism and occupational damage, a line was drawn at the threshold of vandalism: unfair wear and tear was often separately reported by the area building surveyors, and did not appear in the number of incidents.

It was important to known where and when vandalism occurred. The analysis suggested that vandalism is not spread evenly, but affects a few schools repeatedly. Three-quarters of the schools (265) reported no vandalism at all. Of the remaining quarter (81), 75 of the 216 incidents took place at only nine schools.

The vast majority of incidents occurred out of school time, when surveillance was likely to be weakest. Although most schools are fenced in and many have caretakers, there was no evidence that these measures prevented vandalism. They may, however, have reduced it. Only seven schools had intruder alarms fitted, and their record was good. Four had no incidents recorded, and the remaining three had one each.

What emerged most strongly from this analysis was the relationship between the different types of neighbourhood in which schools are set and the incidence of vandalism. Six different types of setting — four urban and two rural — were identified, and the annual cost of repair per 1,000 pupils was calculated for each of them. The results show that over half the cost of repair can be attributed to 24 schools, of which all but one was in an urban setting. In the worst urban areas (areas of poor quality housing) repair costs were eight times heavier than costs in rural areas per head of population.

Any preventive measures will therefore be applied selectively rather than across the board, and as an immediate move Bedfordshire set money aside for intruder alarms and guard dog patrols where they were most needed.

In the longer term, the working party recognised that the threat of vandalism must be taken into account when new schools are being designed. The site must be clearly defined, perhaps by fencing, to make people aware of school limits. To reinforce this, the caretaker's house (if one is provided) should be sited near the entrance to provide a 'presence', with a sufficiently wide view of what is going on around it.

Complete surveillance would demand a layout of unrelieved

dullness. The designer must therefore strike a balance between the need to provide a 'sociable' design, human in scale, reflecting and encouraging a sense of community, and the need to supervise the school grounds. Since the need for supervision is most acute at night, external lighting is suggested as a possible solution. But it is too expensive to be required as a general provision and used indiscriminately. Cost also prohibits the design of truly vandal-proof buildings, if indeed such a design is possible.

Rather than across-the-board solutions – such as the costly strengthening of everything that is likely to get damaged – what is needed is an appreciation of the factors which contribute to wear and tear. Lack of surveillance is one factor. The working party found that unsupervised spaces such as lavatories, cloakrooms and waiting areas along corridors get more than their fair share of damage. Heavy use is

A mixture of wilful damage (graffiti) and poor detailing (the broken door post) in a school lavatory

another: book lockers, cupboards, sanitary fittings, and coat pegs all get very heavy use. Other damage, accidental or not, is concentrated on wall surfaces, convector heaters, doors and windows. Yet raising the performance of components and surfaces may not always be the answer. The working party found that performance of similar components varied widely between one school and another, and could only attribute this to varying conditions in different schools: principally, levels of overcrowding, discipline, and maintenance and general upkeep.

Damage, however trivial and accidental, encourages further damage. The Bedfordshire working party recognised the need for tough, easy-to-maintain materials which could either resist attack or be quickly replaced. Polycarbonate sheet, for example, is now being fitted where normal glazing is repeatedly broken.

But again, the cost of vandal-proofing demands that it be done selectively. The general provision of concealed plumbing, heavy-gauged metal components and unbreakable glass would add considerably to the cost of school buildings, and would not be justified in every case.

The need for external and internal protection presents the designer with the same kind of dilemma as does the need for surveillance. The working party recognised that schools designed for an open type of organisation, in which creative activities link together and share space, present special problems – particularly as they are empty for long periods each day and during long holidays. It is possible to provide only limited physical protection: externally, by fitting of multi-lever security locks to doors and strong catches to windows and rooflights; internally, by providing security stores for valuable goods.

Just as minor damage, unless quickly repaired, encourages further damage, so anything temporary appears to be fair game for vandals. The working party noted that temporary classrooms and buildings got more than their fair share of vandalism, particularly if they were empty or appeared to be derelict. Temporary finishes, too, attract graffiti. The lesson here is that a highly finished permanent building gains greater respect than a makeshift building. Since people *do* seem to respond to elegant, thoughtful appearances, the working party suggests that vandal-resistant materials should be used in a sophisticated manner.

In terms of the damage caused, fire-raising is the most serious kind of vandalism. School fires almost trebled between 1969 and 1974. This increase has been exacerbated by the use in school of new materials which have a low resistance to fire. To reduce the damage the Department of Education and Science has upgraded the provision of fire breaks and fire stops.

The Fire Protection Association recommends the installation of automatic fire alarms in school buildings. Bedfordshire feels that the cost of such a step would be out of all proportion to the scale of its fire problem. However, since it has a policy of equipping isolated or vulnerable schools with intruder alarms, these can be relied on to detect fire raisers as well as ordinary vandals and thieves.

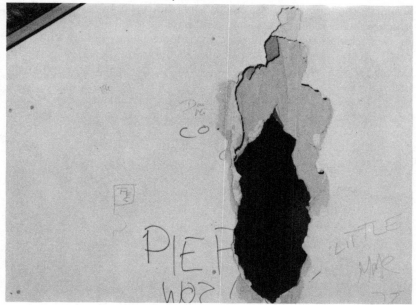

This flimsy walling has provoked more damage than graffiti alone

Fire damage can be very costly to repair

Bedfordshire's approach therefore highlights two areas of constraint when the design of school buildings is considered. The first is financial and the second may be broadly termed social. If vandal-proofing is applied indiscriminately, the costs will outweigh the benefits (though the invisible costs of the disruption of school life which wilful damage causes should perhaps be set alongside the visible costs of maintenance and repair). Even materials and areas which are known to be specifically at risk should be strengthened selectively. Damage reports that identify schools which are repeatedly hit will help such selection.

The social costs of fortifying schools against attack may be even heavier. The design of a school ideally should reinforce a sense of community, defining areas of group activity. The design has to be humane. This is bound to comprise such design features as the ironing out of corners and courtyards made in the interests of easy surveillance. The task is therefore to retain a human scale and a respect for the children who will use the school, while taking commonsense precautions to protect areas or materials which experience has shown to be particularly damage-prone.

For financial and social reasons, local authorities like Bedfordshire are not insisting on designs that resist the worst possible damage. A determined vandal, thief or arsonist will always get through. Instead the aim is to reduce the excuses for casual, rather than premeditated, vandalism and for opportunist, rather than planned, theft.

Accidental damage and temporary-looking or empty premises will, as we have seen, trigger acts of wilful damage. Architects responsible for the design and maintenance of the school buildings of the Inner London Education Authority are quite as worried by recurring minor damage (intentional or accidental) as by the sensational destruction reported in newspapers under the heading of 'Vandalism'.

It is worth considering in detail how the GLC tackles the area of persistent damage where unfair wear and tear (occupational damage) shades into vandalism (wanton destruction), how design can recognise wear and tear and allow generously for it, and how, at the planning stage, protection against theft and vandalism can be included to meet a building's needs.

A two months' study by the GLC maintenance department confirmed that windows, doors and lavatories are the prime targets for vandals. Apart from the cost of repair, replacements for glazing can cause design problems. For example, it is often difficult to obtain replacements for patent colour glasses, laminated panes and glazing units. Poorly matched substitutes defeat the design intentions. Low-level glass in doors and below sills is particularly vulnerable to deliberate (kicking) or accidental (ball games) damage. After several replacements a solid material such as plywood is substituted – again, at the expense of the designer's intentions.

Despite their disadvantages (yellowing, poor resistance to scratching) polycarbonate glazing substitutes are considered the standard solution to the problem of damage-prone glazing. They can also strengthen the security of school buildings. A recent survey of schools showed that there were 637 entries through windows as opposed to 137 through doors. (Over 170 of the window entries were helped by insecure windows.)

Badly sited glazed panels

The average school has a large number of windows, and some security has to be sacrificed to give a light, cheerful atmosphere in school buildings. However, the GLC architects' department suggests in its *Security Design Guide* ways in which the risk of break-ins and resulting vandalism can be reduced at the planning stage. Hinges to opening lights should be fixed so that the hinge pins cannot be taken out from outside the building. All vulnerable windows (for example, ground-floor windows) should have adequate locks. Generally, metal sash or

Screws fastening cover strips in patent glazing are easily removed

centre-pivoted windows are more secure. Louvred windows, the guide points out, are extremely vulnerable and difficult to secure, and should be avoided. Horizontal sliding windows should also be avoided, unless they are fitted with adequate fasteners. In general, all windows and fanlights should be fitted with some sort of mechanical restraint which limits the openings to a maximum of 127mm (5in).

Doors should be solidly built. Lightweight, hollow-cored doors are more easily damaged than solid-cored doors. And although glazed vision panels in doors are a sound idea since they improve surveillance, they should be kept to a minimum size.

Properly designed doors to high-security stores will reduce breakages and subsequent ugly attempts to reinforce them; in practice this means doors lined on the *outside* with sheet metal, fitted with good quality five-lever locks. Cheaper locks can be fitted to classrooms or rooms without a specific security risk. The GLC has found that most doors in school buildings need to be of the same standard as fire doors.

Much of the damage to doors can be reduced at little extra cost simply by recognising what is likely to happen to them in ordinary day-to-day school use. Many doors are damaged by hitting projecting frames, architraves or the edges of reveals when they are opened more than 90 degrees. This can happen when the wind catches at doors on the outside of the building. Adequate and properly located stops or buffers will prevent this. When doors are slammed continually or violently, they can damage the lightweight partitions in which they are set. Storey-height door frames, securely fixed to floor and structural ceiling, can help to prevent this. Lever door handles can be torn off when one child prevents another coming into a room: knobs are preferable.

Lavatories are focal points for vandalism. The design of cloakroom areas illustrates the need for an interplay of management, planning and design decisions. It *is* possible to design a vandal-resistant lavatory. The GLC based its design of a lavatory in the Crystal Palace Sports Centre on the specifications for Borstal lavatories, and it has proved very successful. Architects admit, however, that this was a one-off solution to a particular problem. For school buildings, a less costly, more comprehensive approach is needed. Unsupervised cloakroom areas distributed through a building represent patches of 'indefensible space', a no-man's-land where a sense of responsibility for surroundings is at its lowest. The GLC therefore recommends that, in spite of inconvenience to pupils, lavatories should be centrally located, and staffed by a supervisor who, ideally, should also be responsible for cleaning.

If the actual design of the lavatory cannot prevent damage, the effects of damage should be allowed for. Lavatory floors, the GLC suggests, ought to be able to cope with flooding, by falling to gullies or channels. Ideally, plumbing and cisterns should be tucked away in a locked service duct, which can be reached from outside the lavatory. However, as Bedfordshire points out, the *general* provision of concealed plumbing may be too costly.

The cost-in-use of materials, however, should be considered. Local authorities generally demand that buildings and their furniture should have a design life of 60 years. But there are situations in which a far shorter life should be planned for: where only a building shell is provided, and rooms are added as they are needed (as at Thamesmead), walls do not need to be as strong as a permanent partition wall.

As a general rule, however, initial extra cost is justified over a period of time. Plugs in wash basins soon disappear to be replaced by wads of paper. Blockages and flooding follow. But if a spray tap dispensing blended water is installed initially it soon repays the higher original outlay. Conventional WC pans are quickly demolished, so stainless steel pans are worth considering.

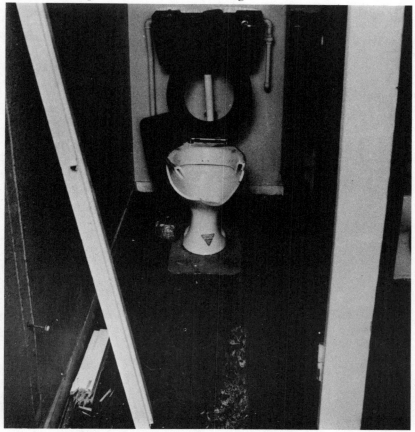

This lavatory might have lasted longer if a stainless steel unit had been used

Within the building, the GLC's approach is to concentrate on the detailing of three or four key areas to reduce the opportunities for vandalism. Protection of the outside, particularly from juvenile break-ins, is tackled rather more broadly. Ten crimes a day are reported in schools every day of the year. About 10 per cent of these are identifiable break-ins, resulting in either the pilfering of school equipment or vandalism. This is opportunist rather than professional, and can be deterred by commonsense precautions at the design stage of a building.

Where supervision is good — for example where the sides of buildings are overlooked by the schoolkeeper's house — break-ins are rare. Therefore the schoolkeeper's house should be sited to give supervision of main entrances and as much of the building as possible. The school building should also relate to the community, so that neighbours can supervise by overlooking the schoolkeeper's entrances.

There is a relationship between the design of school buildings and their vulnerability. The GLC architects emphasise that the very shape of buildings is critical to the degree of security, particularly in single-storey buildings. Concealed internal courts are particularly vulnerable and need a high degree of security in detailing doors and windows. Detailing can sometimes aid break-ins. The stepping of flat roofs and rooflights can act as a ladder, and deep recesses and reveals can act as a shield. Open-plan designs used in recent buildings make surveillance by police and public much easier.

Schools are particularly vulnerable because the children's sense of belonging to any one part of them is weak: children move from classroom to classroom with each lesson instead of remaining in one classroom which they can regard as their own, visited by a succession of teachers. This constant circulation is obviously outside the designer's control. But the kind of precautions suggested above balance the need for a 'humane' building with the requirement for a secure one.

Vandal-resistant equipment and detail design

by Jane Sykes, Design Council

Vandalism is a very prevalent crime: approximately 306,300 offences of criminal damage were reported in England and Wales in 1978 according to Home Office figures. It costs an increasing amount of money each year to put things right. But the cost of vandalism cannot only be reckoned in monetary terms. Repairing wilful damage is a waste of time and resources which could be employed more positively, but until repairs can be effected hardship and inconvenience may have to be endured.

Vandalism can contribute to or cause accidents: a broken public telephone by failing to be the means of summoning help to a car crash could be the indirect cause of death; a damaged slide in a playground could cause serious injury to children. An area that shows signs of persistent vandalism has a rundown and depressing appearance that lowers the morale of residents and encourages further vandalism.

The designer and the specifier of equipment cannot alone hope to eradicate a problem whose roots must lie in society and the attitudes of its members, but careful design and choice of equipment can help to minimise the effects of vandalism. This section is not concerned with the wider design aspects of planning public housing or schools (covered by David White in his sections) but with detail. The layout of a school by providing good surveillance can deter the writer of graffiti, so also can a special wall covering or vandal-resistant surface. A caretaker in a well planned school may be able to keep an eye on the main entrances, but window locks at the back and an intruder alarm could help him to maintain security.

The choice of special equipment will be governed by cost and appropriateness, two things that go logically together. It would be, for example, both expensive and inappropriate to fit an old people's home with vandal-proof lavatories. Despite the high initial cost, such lavatories could save money in the long run if fitted in a borstal or public lavatory in a vandal-prone area. Similarly the judicious use of special glazing can save trouble and money in particularly vandal- or accident-prone settings (ground-level glass panels, windows in sports complexes and so on) while wholesale use would be unnecessary and expensive. Again, in some areas where schools are regularly broken into an intruder alarm might be worth considering, particularly if arson were a possibility. Strong locks alone might be adequate protection, however, for a school in a quiet country district, and money that would have been needed for the purchase, installation and servicing of an alarm could be devoted to other purposes.

Vandalism covers a broad spectrum of activities from the trivial but tiresome to the really serious, from graffiti writing to crimes leading to arson. Vandalism is usually associated with other crimes, in particular petty theft, and can be committed in the course of another crime: breaking and entering can be accompanied by wilful damage especially if the thieves are frustrated in their search for valuables. It is worth while taking measures to protect property: the police in the form of the local Crime Prevention Officer are always willing to advise and they have great experience. They will advise both large organisations and the individual.

Graffiti

Once a vandal had to carry a bucket of whitewash and a large brush to write legends on walls – inconvenient and noticeable. Now things are much easier for him: he can carry around a neat pocket-sized aerosol of paint or for smaller messages use a modest felt-tip pen. Although they can be witty, graffiti can also be crude, unsightly and even politically and racially inflammatory. Removal, or even better still prevention, is desirable.

One method of discouragement is to apply approved 'graffiti' in the form of murals or mosaics on what might be tempting surfaces if undecorated. These serve the dual function of protecting the surface and more importantly of giving interest and colour in areas that might otherwise appear dully uniform. They can vary from the magnificent professionally inspired town art of Glenrothes to more informal murals painted by local children.

But murals are by no means suitable in all cases, so surfaces have to be protected in other ways. It is wise when planning wall finishes to avoid a soft-textured one which can be easily scratched, particularly if

BUILDING RESEARCH STATION

The light substrate makes these graffiti easy to write (or scratch)

70

the surface colour contrasts with that of the substrate. Light colours are also best avoided. If a surface is chosen that will need to be renewed it is unwise to choose one that will be too expensive for frequent renewal.

There are ways of producing a deliberately vandal-proof surface besides taking the commonsense precautions above to minimise temptation and potential damage. Interior surfaces in such places as public conveniences and subways that are open to the public but where a vandal may enjoy a certain amount of privacy are an ideal target. Their walls can be covered with tough glazed ceramic tiles: special vandal-proof tiles are available that will not readily mark or scratch and present an attractive appearance. Plastics laminates can be used as

LANGLEY LONDON LTD

Langley London Ltd produce these tiles which give a pleasant but vandal-resistant finish. Here they are used inside a block of flats

panels to protect surfaces. For both internal and external surfaces special non-stick (and so non-mark) paints and coatings are available based on polyurethanes such as fluorocarbonates. There are also cheaper easy-to-clean coatings based on vinyls, but these do not last as long as the polyurethanes. Some of the firms that make these coatings also manufacture special solvents for removing graffiti in any medium from paint to lipstick, felt tip to oil, both from their own special easy-to-clean surfaces and from untreated surfaces. A cold-water high-pressure washer may be needed together with a special solvent to remove paint which has sunk into concrete or brick.

Buildings can be constructed with surfaces that resist damage and marking such as ribbed metal sheet, rough-textured bricks or a rough-cast surface. These are tough and not particularly inviting to the vandal, but unlike some of the specially designed vandal-proof coatings, are not easy to clean. It can also happen in some cases that a really tough surface acts as a challenge to vandals.

Lighting

Good lighting – in the street, in the corridors and staircases of public housing, in car-parks and subways and around the perimeters of industrial sites – acts as a deterrent both to vandals and to other criminals. But its nature and its permanent unguarded presence make it a common target for attack itself. There are three main factors in protecting lighting equipment – siting, maintenance and construction of the equipment itself, bearing in mind that the luminaire and the doors to control gear compartments in columns are the vulnerable parts.

It is ideal to put luminaires out of reach of vandals, either by using tall columns or by attaching them high up the walls of buildings. But this is not always possible and will not necessarily provide the right kind of illumination for an area that may need the supplement of less impersonal low-level lighting, for alleys and steps where wall-mounted units may not give adequate light at ground level. Columns should not be sited near walls or low buildings where they can be readily climbed and used for access to property or other equipment. Nor should equipment be sited in hidden corners or behind buildings where it could be easily tampered with unseen.

If lighting is not regularly and systematically checked and re-paired, its deterrent effect will not only be reduced but slight accidental damage will encourage more serious wilful damage and the air of decay given by faulty equipment will lead to a general lack of care by the people using the area.

The actual equipment needs to be sturdy and durable with the sort of finish that is not easily marked or scratched. The materials used should not corrode, nor be readily bent or deformed and fixings should be hidden where possible, leaving nothing that can be torn off or opened up. Doors protecting the control gear on the bottom of columns are particularly susceptible to being prised open and since the control gear is expensive this is a major disadvantage. Certain lanterns are made with the control gear incorporated into them and comparatively safe from interference: these are for mounting on a plain pole. The use of column doors can also be avoided by housing the control gear for a

This pedestrian underpass links two housing estates. The open, well lit design was deliberately planned by Warrington Development Corporation to give confidence to users, especially at night. The lighting fittings were chosen for their ability to stand up to vandalism: they are fitted flush in a cast in situ concrete trough at the top of the side slopes; the gap to the soffit of the beams is big enough to open the units for maintenance but does not allow enough space for anyone using a hammer or crowbar to operate effectively

group of lamp standards separately in a specially designed tamperproof unit. Glass luminaires will break if vigorously attacked, but glass can be replaced with tough plastics materials such as polycarbonate. Some manufacturers offer the option of a polycarbonate globe, while some items are designed using polycarbonate or other plastics with different degrees of strength, as a standard feature. Items such as bulkhead luminaires whose positioning puts them at risk are designed in vandal-proof versions.

DESIGN COUNCIL

The door in this lamp standard has been broken, but the makeshift method of repair leaves a wide gap into which a bar could easily be inserted to prise it open once again

Security lighting for protecting factories and industrial sites is in a slightly different category from street lighting in that it serves only a deterrent purpose and is not a public amenity. Its primary purpose is to deter thieves – or catch them before they can steal anything – but since vandals are attracted by industrial sites, particularly if construction is going on, and can be responsible for costly damage, it serves a dual function. The lighting columns can usually be located inside the perimeter fence where there is one, but if wall-mounted luminaires or

This GEC lantern has a polycarbonate sphere moulded in one piece to resist attack; it is the ZD 4542 post top lantern

floodlights have to be used in an unprotected position vandal-proof models should be used. Such lighting should be arranged to deter intruders; should intruders not be deterred, lighting should be designed to reveal their presence to a guard or patrolling policeman. In turn, security lighting should be directed so that the position of guards and nightwatchmen can be concealed. The first objective is achieved by producing a glare directed towards the perimeter fence so that an intruder will be dazzled and feel vulnerable since he will be unable to tell whether or not a guard inside is watching him. The second is achieved by lighting vertical surfaces such as walls or fences brightly so that the dark figures of intruders will be clearly visible. The third is the corollary of the first, the guard can watch the perimeter fence without himself being observed. Gates and access points need special treatment as entry may be attempted here if the deterrent effect of the perimeter lighting is successful. The Electricity Council produces a booklet called *Essentials of Security Lighting* (A Guide for Industry and Commerce) which gives clear and detailed advice.

Street furniture other than lighting units

The same basic principles apply to street furniture in general as to lighting in particular allowing for differences in use: strong construction; good surfaces; non-corrodible materials and fixings; hidden fastenings; avoidance of any projecting or easily removable parts; sensible siting; regular maintenance. A final, but vital, design feature is that equipment should be easy to repair. When items of street furniture become redundant they should be removed at once. With some items, such as street signs, damage can be prevented by putting them out of reach, for example on high poles or on the side of buildings. Vandal-resistant plastics can be used for glazing in items like bus shelters and illuminated bollards, also for traffic lights and the globes of belisha beacons. Some items by their very nature must be accessible to the public – litter bins, seats, parking meters. As in the case of lighting columns these should be carefully sited, so that there is no chance of their providing convenient ways of climbing walls or on to buildings. Although all the general points apply, maintenance and upkeep are especially important. Nothing gives a rundown appearance more quickly than seatless benches and overflowing litter bins. Many litter bins are designed with a separate lining for easy emptying and these can usually be padlocked to the outer casing. In areas where the incidence of vandalism is high it is worth replacing conventional litter bins with those made in vandal-resistant materials and checking that where they are attached to lamp-posts extra strong steel bands are used. Furniture that is ground fixed – seats, litter bins, pedestrian guard-rails

This bollard, Decagon from Concrete Utilities Ltd, is designed to be vandal-proof. The lighting mechanism is protected by a locked aluminium plate on the top. The light shines through polycarbonate behind the tapered slits

etc — should be fixed in the ground at a reasonable depth and the pavement or road surfacing round them should be properly finished off to discourage disturbance. Furniture that is not ground fixed should be too heavy to be readily removed. Parking meters are tempting to petty thieves: they should have flush-fitting doors which allow no gap into which something could be forced to lever them open; the doors should have hidden internal hinges and a tamperproof lock; they should be in a strong material to resist attack. If one meter in a row is successfully attacked, the way that it works will be revealed and the rest of the row will be broken open and robbed within a very short space of time. Planting is liable to vandalism and using raised beds or planters can prevent people taking shortcuts over planted areas. If the plants chosen are dense and prickly they are less likely to be interfered with than those that are pleasant to touch – conversely should litter be thrown among them it will be more difficult to clear.

Telephone boxes have been a popular target for vandals for a long time. The Post Office has done a great deal to strengthen boxes and has seen as a result a steady improvement in equipment remaining functional. Some of the main elements in new boxes have been the replacement of glass with steel plates in the lower windows and with polycarbonate above, the use of all-steel coinbox equipment, strengthened handsets with steel conductor cords, recessed dials which are difficult to remove and 24-hour fluorescent lighting.

Vending machines

Like parking meters and public telephones, vending machines can arouse the cupidity of the petty thief as well as the aggression of the vandal. Many machines, however, are never attacked at all: these are usually situated in semi-private settings such as in factories or offices where they are used regularly by the same people. Here it would be entirely self-defeating to put them out of action; but also should a machine fail to function properly, in particular by taking in money but not sending out goods, the customer would know to whom to complain. Where machines are sited in the street or at a railway station it is not so easy to get redress. A certain amount of vandalism may well be generated by frustration with malfunctioning machines. So all machines should carry an operator's name, address and telephone number as one step to relieve this frustration. Similarly they should be regularly checked for damage and for refilling to ensure they continue to give the service for which they are intended. Sometimes something as simple as the powders for hot drinks clogging up inside the machine can put it out of action and this could be quickly solved in a regular cleaning and refilling check. Ideally the coin mechanism should be readily replaceable as one of the most effective ways of vandalising a machine is to stick chewing gum in the coin slot. Otherwise the general comments for street furniture apply – sturdy construction, sensible siting and so on. There is a trade association – the Automatic Vending Association of Britain, 50 Eden Street, Kingston-upon-Thames, Surrey – which could give further details about manufacturers in this field.

A common fate for vending machines

Lavatories and public conveniences

It is not only public lavatories that are affected by vandalism – schools, motorway cafés, factories, some pubs and offices all suffer to a greater or lesser degree. The points David White makes on p 66 about school lavatories apply generally. The employment of a supervisor is desirable, but much can be done by design alone. Since lavatories are notorious for their graffiti, the section on this form of vandalism is particularly relevant. Exposed pipes are vulnerable and damage to them specially destructive with resulting flooding, so all piping should be hidden behind strong panels with tamperproof fastenings. Pre-plumbed sanitary units designed so that piping can easily be concealed are available. A locked door, preferably outside the lavatory itself, should give access to the plumbing for maintenance. If sanitary units are continually smashed – or if research suggests that they might be in a new installation – it would be economic to fit stainless steel units. These are fabricated as one piece to resist attack, and of course will not smash or crack. Since sinks are liable to become blocked either accidentally from careless treatment or deliberately, the installation of spray taps – and the removal of plugs – and channels in the floor designed to drain off excess water are useful precautions. The replacement of towels with electrically operated hand dryers removes another potential problem, as do soap dispensers housed in close fitting cowls attached to the wall with concealed fixings. Lavatory paper is often pilfered and can constitute an item of considerable expenditure. To combat this problem jumbo-sized rolls with weights of between 2kg and 3kg are available and are difficult to remove without attracting attention.

W & G SISSONS LTD

Part of a range of stainless steel sanitary ware made by W & G Sissons Ltd. Its attractive clean lines offer a strong smooth surface to resist attack

It may be necessary to provide ashtrays where more than a basic washbasin is fitted, in particular where the basins are surrounded by a plastics-covered surface. This can be damaged by cigarette burns through carelessness as much as deliberate vandalism. But the ashtrays themselves may prove a temptation to petty thieves and vandals and should only be used in lavatories with an attendant. Where there is no attendant surfaces should be planned that do not burn: ceramic tiles can replace plastics.

Coat hooks are popular targets. The best mitigation of the problem is the use of hidden fastenings and sturdy designs, but these will not necessarily solve the problem.

Housing

David White's section on p 43 covers the general approach to planning public housing, but detail is important too. Vandals chipped away the concrete surface of one of the columns supporting a high-rise block of flats. This exposed the steel reinforcement inside the column to the elements. Had the maintenance not been good – it was, the damage being quickly seen, noted as serious and action taken – the steel would have corroded and eventually the main structure of the flats would have been seriously affected. Surfaces are more important than they might seem. Vital structural elements should be carefully protected: this can be done by cladding concrete with steel or a strong sheeting material provided that the method of fastening does not lend itself to vandalism. An expensive but effective alternative used in Scandinavia is to cast tiles into the concrete at the time of building. Soft mortar in brickwork can easily be scraped out, so joints should be regularly inspected and deteriorated mortar mix raked out and replaced by a good quality mix of sand and cement. Glazing and tile-hung walls below ground-floor window level are particularly liable to damage and are best avoided. Piping, whether lead or copper, should be installed inside a building and not out, since it is tempting to petty thieves. Drain pipes should be cast iron rather than plastics or asbestos-cement below the height of 2m; they should be built up with concrete so that they cannot be wrenched off the building nor can the brackets fixing them be used as footholds by anyone trying to climb them. Ground-floor windows may be constantly broken if they face on to an area where children play and it may be worth replacing ordinary window glass with toughened glass, which will probably stand up to being bumped by a football although not to a deliberate attempt to smash it. (It is also well suited for use in glass doors and other vulnerable locations where breakage may be due to carelessness as much as to deliberate destructiveness.) Plastics glazing such as that using polycarbonate is very strong and can be suitable for certain applications, but it is expensive, needs special window fittings since it expands and contracts and can be considerably defaced by scratching. In certain cases ground-floor and semi-basement windows can be barred; this is suitable if they light a garage or store, but is not so desirable in living quarters. It is wise to provide window locks.

Locks and security might appear important only in deterring thieves and to have no relevance to vandals. But petty theft and vandalism are often closely allied and as mentioned before a frustrated thief may turn into a vengeful wrecker. So houses should be equipped with a good quality mortice deadlock to BS 3621 if possible. This should be situated at least 40mm away from the letter box and well clear of any glazing. If there is a strip of glazing protect it with a decorative grille so that no would-be intruder can break the glass, put his hand in and open the door. Clearly the door itself should be strong enough to withstand being kicked: the use of soft core doors intended as internal doors as the exterior doors of flats will not give adequate protection however good the locks. Exterior doors not used as final exit doors, for example the back doors of houses, should be provided with strong bolts, top and bottom: mortice-bolts are best since surface-mounted bolts are only as strong as the screws that hold them. French doors are particularly vulnerable: the best protection for them is to fit mortice security bolts at the top and bottom of the first closing leaf and to fit a two-bolt mortice lock – preferably of the hook or clutch type – to the final closing leaf. Louvre windows are difficult to protect and are best avoided in a position where they could easily be forced by an intruder. Not only should ground-floor windows have locks but also any window near a flat roof, balcony or any possible access point. Many kinds of window lock are available, including those that lock the window open to give ventilation but not widely enough to give access; the most secure window locks have separate keys. Old people and people living alone are wise to have door chains and possibly door viewers in their front doors. The local Crime Prevention Officer can provide fuller and more detailed advice. Insurance companies will often advise their clients and may indeed insist on certain precautions.

Since much vandalism occurs actually inside blocks of flats in the communal areas and is often perpetrated by people who are not residents some local authorities and most privately owned blocks use an Entryphone to make casual entry difficult. Even without an Entryphone certain precautions can be taken. Individual flats can be secured as suggested above. Graffiti writing can be discouraged by the use of the kinds of product mentioned under the heading 'Graffiti'. Lighting can be protected by the use of polycarbonates and hidden fixings and the visitor's WC can be protected like any public lavatory. The reason for the provision of the latter is itself an anti-vandal measure: in some blocks where no WC is available the lifts have been fouled.

Lifts are vital to life in tall buildings and are frequently attacked. It is now possible to install vandal-proof lifts, or, if the potential damage does not warrant so extreme a reaction, a vandal-resistant push-button system for lifts. The success of these designs is based on leaving nothing to chance. The vandal is presented with an attractive product with no gaps, projections, breakable or markable surfaces or thin easily de-formed parts. There is more than one of these special lifts on the market. The following details apply to the Wadsworth lift, but the same principles obtain for vandal-proof lifts in general. The lift is finished in light-gauge chequerplate treated with acid-resistant primer and then painted; its floor is covered in epoxy resin trowelled to the sides to form a seal; the 3mm-thick steel doors have a built-in safety tongue on the bottom track; vision panels are just large enough for their purpose but too small to be attacked with hammer blows and are a sandwich of polycarbonate sheeting and Georgian-style wired glass; ventilation points are inconspicuous. The whole lift car is well lighted (always a deterrent) by a light fitted with polycarbonate cover and accessible only from the car roof. The buttons are designed to be resistant to jamming and to cigarette lighter flames. Indicators are polycarbonate. The push-button system similarly is designed to offer no possible opening to the vandal: its stainless steel escutcheon is secured by concealed fasteners; the buttons are moulded into red-tinted polycarbonate lenses and so designed that shock loads are absorbed by the body and not by the contacts, and so that there is no space round the buttons into which match sticks or similar objects can be forced.

DEWHURST & PARTNER LTD

The Dupar US80 illuminated push-button system from Dewhurst & Partner Ltd has been specifically designed to be vandal proof
Right: the system successfully resists attack

Finally, as with every other aspect of this subject, maintenance is very important. Apparent lack of care in local authorities and landlords encourages carelessness in tenants and passers-by and before long deliberate damage.

Garages

Ideally garages should be overlooked by houses or flats, but not so near them as to provide an easy way of climbing up the buildings. Windows are better avoided since even if these are too small to climb through, they can still be broken and paint or missiles thrown through on to the car inside. Windows in doors are open to the same objection and weaken the door. Garage roofs are not usually particularly strong – they are often of asbestos cement – which means they will serve their purpose adequately, but may not bear the weight of climbing children or of objects hurled up on to them (which they were not designed to do). For this reason any feature that may help a child (or an adult) to reach the roof should be avoided – conveniently sited handles, drain-pipes, cills and so on. The roof can be positively protected by wide projections at the eaves if it is sloping or at the edge if it is flat. Parapet walls could be also be used. These precautions would be appropriate for any low roof, not just for garages.

Up-and-over doors must be of adequate strength since children swinging on them could distort them and dislocate the balancing mechanism. If doors of this type are used they should be heavy versions with a lock at floor level to resist attempts to kick the door in. Perhaps an even better door would be one that was heavy-framed, ledged and braced and fitted with a padlock and stout hasp and staple. A specially designed vandal-proof door is produced made of heavy-gauge galvan-ised steel; it has a four-point locking system with locking bars in each corner; the lock is retractable and fits flush with the door when closed.

Empty property and building sites

Empty shops and houses are a great temptation to children and among them to potential vandals. One broken window can serve as a trigger for all out attack on a property over a very short space of time. So if it is possible, empty premises should be boarded up immediately – this can

A neatly fenced building site, with a cabin well placed for surveillance. Lighting has been provided where the scaffolding overhangs the pavement. Good lighting is a vital feature in deterring vandalism

be done neatly and securely with sawn timber planks creosoted without creating an eyesore. Similarly building sites attract children: apparent chaos may make ownership of the objects there seem diffuse. These can be protected by high close-boarded fencing with viewing panels so that the site can be seen by passers-by and patrolling policemen. Where the building project is a long-term one it might be worth investing in higher grade fencing.

Shops

This is another area where protection is primarily against thieves, but vandals can do a lot of damage. The window can be protected with special glazing, but is most secure if covered with a lockable grille at night. If a grille is not used internal lighting has a deterrent effect. Rear windows should be barred or glass window bricks can be used, but these can be smashed. The back door should open outwards, be protected by metal sheeting on the outside, be fitted with hinge bolts and if possible be recessed into the wall. A safe and an alarm (see under 'Schools' below) should be considered. The front door should have a lock to BS 3621 or a close shackle padlock and suitable hasp and staple or locking bar. If the shop sells milk or drinks, crates of empty bottles should be left inside the shop, not outside where they might make convenient missiles for vandals.

Schools

By their very nature schools are a primary target for vandalism. Their layout is well known and for many hours they are empty, besides which when in use they are occupied by large numbers of the age groups most prone to vandalism. David White's section on page 59 looks at the problem in general, but as in other areas aspects of detailed design can help. Many of the comments above on such things as preventing graffiti, design of lavatories and glazing are relevant to schools. Design detail in the exterior of the building can encourage or hinder vandals. Projections, ledges, convenient drainpipes, flat roofs of buildings arranged in steps, hidden courtyards and corners, all these are aids to entry: avoided, entry is more difficult. But security is bound to be a problem in a building whose function demands that it is not designed like a prison and where there are limited funds for imposing a high degree of security. External doors should of course be strong and fitted with locks to BS 3621, but the majority of break-ins are effected through windows. In extreme cases glass can be replaced by special plastics glazing – which serves the dual function of preventing breakages and inhibiting entry – but this is expensive and the way that polycarbonate can be scratched usually rules it out for secondary schools: it can provide too convenient a surface for graffiti writing. Toughened glass used throughout a school can have the same effect as in housing, preventing accidental damage. Window locks should be used. It is advised that ground-floor windows are designed so that they do not open at the bottom but ventilation is provided by small lights in the top of the window. Since grilles over windows and bars while effective may be socially undesirable these are not an ideal solution. Window frames like those of the traditional Georgian window which are designed for small panes of glass can act like a set of bars without giving an offputting appearance. The frame must be of a strong material and the space left for the panes too small for even a young child to squeeze through. There is an added advantage in that if one small pane is broken the cost of replacement is considerably less than where very large panes of glass are used. Rooflights should not be forgotten in considering security: the most secure are of polycarbonate and their fixings are inside. External screws are easily undone.

A clutch head screw from Guest Keen & Nettlefold Ltd. Its head is designed so that it can be fastened easily with a flat blade screwdriver in the normal way, but is virtually impossible to undo

All schools have expensive items of equipment: instead of leaving these scattered about the school in insecure classrooms they can be collected in the evening and put into a storeroom designed for the purpose. This room can have a barred window, steel-lined door and special lock. Similarly sophisticated locks can be fitted to key rooms like the headmaster's study and secretary's office, while classrooms may have lockable cupboards for comparatively low value items and no door locks at all. In this way the best security can be supplied where it is needed without the high cost of a blanket of expensive security.

Assuming that someone will be bound to get in despite moderate precautions, there is more that can be done to minimise damage. Power supplies should be turned off in such places as laboratories where Bunsen burners might be played with and could cause a fire. Similar action should be taken in workshops where there is potentially dangerous equipment.

If a school suffers from continual vandalism an intruder alarm may be necessary. An alarm may well scare off children before they can do much damage, or it can summon help so that vandals can be apprehended quickly. But there are disadvantages: fewer than five per cent of alarm calls are genuine which means that the police and school keyholder are frequently unnecessarily disturbed; alarm systems are expensive and the costs continue after the initial capital outlay, since they must be serviced regularly; alarms themselves can encourage misbehaviour in children, who soon learn how to set them off.

There is a British Standard for intruder alarm systems in buildings, BS 4737, which specifies the construction, operation, installation, maintenance and detailed requirements for detection devices. Rapid advances in technology since the standard was first published in 1971 have resulted in its being completely revised into a multi-section edition. Over a hundred companies that install alarm systems belong to the National Supervisory Council for Intruder Alarms, a body that guarantees that its members' alarm systems comply with BS 4737 and in accordance with the standard undertakes through its inspectorate that its alarms will be in good working order. There are also alarms complying with BS 4737 that are not made by members of the NSCIA.

There are various different kinds of alarm system, ranging from the simple to the very complex. The silent alarm types include: direct lines connected to alarm companies' central stations or to police stations; automatic dialling (a 999 call); digital diallers or other types which could ring in a caretaker's house. All these systems can be fitted with delayed-action self-actuating external audible alarms (usually a bell). Some systems have an audible alarm only. The triggering devices available are of various different kinds too:

o continuous wiring – a break in the wiring triggers the alarm
o foil on glass – the foil forms part of an electric circuit and if the glass is cracked the foil will fracture breaking the circuit and triggering the alarm
o protective switches – these are placed on doors and windows and the corresponding frame; should the door or window be opened the contact will be broken and the alarm triggered
o microwave detectors – these give 'trap' protection: a certain area is covered with microwaves by an electronic device and

monitored by a receiver; movement within the area will disturb the waves which will be registered by the receiver and the alarm will be triggered

o ultrasonic – similar to the above using waves of a lower frequency

o acoustic – similar to the above using waves of a still lower frequency; probably not suitable for schools since the system is designed to react to noise and is best used in a strong room or similar place where there should be no noise whatsoever

o passive infra-red – similar again, but a rise in temperature is what causes the alarm to be triggered

o volumetric capacitive detectors – probably not suitable for schools. These must be used for a sealed area. The alarm is triggered by a change of volume in the area

o pressure mats – mats are placed at possible access points and a change of pressure as when someone steps on one breaks the circuit and triggers the alarm

o vibration detectors – devices set to register vibration. When vibration increases beyond a certain limit the alarm is triggered

o rigid printed circuits – an electronic device, often used in gun cupboards

o beam interruption detector – a beam is sent from a transmitter to a receiver and the alarm is triggered when the beam is disturbed as when someone walks through it

o capacitive proximity detectors – devices that register an increase in capacity when, for example, a person approaches one; this is programmed to trigger the alarm; these devices are probably not suitable for schools

o deliberately operated devices – panic buttons etc, suitable for banks and for certain domestic uses, probably not suitable for schools

As this brief listing implies, alarm systems can be very complex and some sophisticated systems are available built up from the kind of elements listed above and incorporating closed circuit television. These are for places (probably not schools) that need a high degree of security and will be used in conjunction with a team of guards. The potential danger and the degree of protection needed will dictate the complexity of the system necessary.

As all this indicates, alarm systems are a specialist area calling for expert knowledge. The Crime Prevention Officer from the local police force can supply this and most security firms will do a free survey and advise on the best kind of system for the particular job.

Vandals can cause fires, but since an intruder alarm should give warning of their presence in a building, fire alarms, although important, are outside the scope of this book.

Factories and industrial sites

The precautions taken to protect industrial premises against thieves serve also to deter vandals. Security lighting, alarms, locks and so on have been discussed already in other contexts but are all relevant. Guard dogs and security patrols are outside the scope of this book, but perhaps a brief mention should be made of fencing. BS 1722: Part 10 : 1972 covers anti-intruder chain link fencing. As with security lighting, if the perimeter is well defended it is important to have good security at gates and entrances. In the fencing itself joins and fastenings are the most vulnerable points; the strongest fencing is weak if it is secured to supporting posts with loops of wire that can be easily undone or cut, or might serve as a foothold to someone climbing the fence. Special rivets can be used in place of wire.

Warning notices

A final possible deterrent to vandalism can be made by warning potential vandals that certain acts may evoke penalties – such as a fine for dropping litter – or may put the perpetrator in danger – such as touching a pylon. Warning signs could be particularly important when it is realised that an adventurous teenager may climb over high walls and fences and expose himself to dangers that he might be expected to be protected from by the wall or fence. Obviously warning signs must be clear and unambiguous. Many people who commit acts of vandalism are very young, or if older tend to be non-achievers at school, so may have difficulty reading or even be illiterate. Pictorial road signs as used on the Continent have been in use in Britain since 1963. Work is now going on into pictorial signs for use in the work place which will include warning notices. The Health and Safety Executive is in the process of drawing up Safety Signs and Colours Regulations which will be used in conjunction with BS 5378: Part 1 an up-dated version of the existing standard: a consultative document will be produced before the regulations are finalised. The regulations will be specifically for the work place, but could be very useful elsewhere.

Children's playgrounds

by Paul Burall, Design Council

Equipment in children's playgrounds can be especially vulnerable to vandalism, not least because they are places where children are expected to congregate and because they are often in open parks which are badly lit and little frequented by the public at night. What is more, vandalism in playgrounds can lead to tragic accidents. There have been cases of swings collapsing after bolts have been removed. In one instance a piece of the surface of a slide was prised up, and subsequently gouged through the thigh of a young girl using the slide. There have even been instances of razor blades and nails being inserted deliberately in the gaps between sections of a slide.

Some of these potential hazards can be avoided by using modern and well designed equipment: the relevant British Standard is BS 5696 : 1979. For example, slides can now be manufactured in one continuous strip, leaving no gaps for vandals to attack. A slide that follows the contour of a mound or runs down a playhouse roof does not require steps or handrails to stop children falling, as it is impossible to fall vertically for any distance; this also removes another target for the vandals.

Some general advice can be given for other items of playground equipment. First, all fixings and fastenings should, wherever possible, be completely hidden; if this is not possible, then they should be of a type that requires a special tool to loosen them. Second, all moving parts should be protected in a way that prevents covers being prised off or otherwise easily removed. Third, materials should be as strong as possible, for example, the kind of glass fibre playthings suitable for supervised playgroups are totally unsuited to a public park. Finally, certain kinds of amenity just should not be used unless there is full-time supervision while the playground is open and proper security when it is closed: paddling pools in particular are a temptation for vandals armed with a bottle, and broken glass is not just dangerous but is difficult to remove.

Safety surfaces beneath certain kinds of equipment from which there is a danger of falls are becoming more widespread as a useful way of alleviating injuries when the inevitable accident does happen. But not all surfaces are suitable for all environments. One approach is to use one of the special cellular rubber surfaces which are now available. These can be used in unsupervised areas but are expensive. An alternative that has been tried successfully in Warrington is to place the whole playground about 30 centimetres below the level of the surrounding area and to fill the hollow with a thick layer of 'Leca' or similar lightweight aggregate. This absorbs energy satisfactorily, is weather-resistant, does not hurt if thrown around, and, if the playground is surrounded by a wide path, just needs occasional sweeping back into the hollow to maintain it.

But perhaps the most important advice is to ensure that all playground equipment is inspected visually for defects, preferably every morning in vandal-prone areas and once a week or once a month elsewhere. A check of accident records in a number of hospitals throughout Britain suggests that between 20,000 and 40,000 children require hospital treatment each year as a result of accidents involving playground equipment, and many of these accidents are caused either by vandalism or by the over exuberant use of equipment. Climbing frames have fallen on children after bolts have been removed; a broken plank on one roundabout caused five broken ankles before it was repaired; one child broke his back after falling through the vandalised platform of a tower slide. All of these defects would have been obvious to any maintenance staff looking for them, and the injuries were, therefore, unnecessary.

It would take no skill at all to see that this roundabout is dangerous

Appendix of manufacturers

In Design Council books it is usual to refer to products which have been accepted for Design Index, the Design Council's register of well designed British goods. The Index covers street furniture and equipment for parks including playground equipment: this part of the Index is published in two catalogues *Street Furniture* and *Equipment for Parks and Amenity Areas* available from the Design Centre Bookshop. These catalogues list well designed street furniture, but users should consult the manufacturers about specifically vandal-resistant models. Other relevant equipment is not covered by the Index and as it would be unhelpful to say that equipment is available without suggesting where it might be obtained a list of manufacturers is included. This list is by no means exhaustive and the products from the manufacturers included have not been seen by Design Council Selection Committees as there is at the moment no suitable category in the Index. There is a security division, but this concentrates mainly on domestic security and while helpful on such things as window locks, will not help on complex alarm systems for public buildings. The local Crime Prevention Officer is the best guide here. He will know the local security firms and using a local firm may be important since alarms need regular servicing and should be planned to fit the peculiar needs of the building which they are to protect. He can of course also advise on locks. Insurance companies will also be helpful over the kind and degree of security to provide.

Security glazing

The Glass and Glazing Federation, 6 Mount Row, London W1Y 6DU (telephone number 01-629 8334) produce lists of their members giving details of what they produce, including safety glass, polycarbonates and other plastics glazing.

Graffiti

Armourclad Ltd
Armourclad House, 5/6 West Park
Harrogate, North Yorkshire
Telephone Harrogate 60657
Special coating

Camrex Special Coating Services Ltd
Camrex House, PO Box 34
Sunderland SR1 2QA
Telephone Sunderland 70811
Special coatings; graffiti remover suitable for treated and untreated surfaces

Dimex Ltd
Dimex House, 116 High Street
Solihull, West Midlands B91 3SD
Telephone 021-704 3551/2/3/4
Graffiti remover suitable for treated and untreated surfaces

England Hughes Bell & Co Ltd
Valley Works, Monton Road
Eccles, Manchester M30 9HJ
Telephone 061-789 5191
Special paint; remover suitable for treated and untreated surfaces

Jet Industrial (Miamead) Ltd
Industrial House
122/124 Pemberton Road, London N4 1BA
Telephone 01-348 0592/01-340 3588
Special coatings; graffiti removers suitable for treated and untreated surfaces; a complete cleaning service offered

Langley London Ltd
The Tile Centre
161-3-5-7 Borough High Street
London SE1 1HU
Telephone 01-407 4444
Vandal-resistant tiles

National Chemsearch (UK) Ltd
Ryders Green Road
West Bromwich, West Midlands
Telephone 021-525 1666
Graffiti removers suitable for treated and untreated surfaces

Planlight Chemicals Ltd
29/31 High Street, Great Bookham
Surrey
Telephone Bookham 52087
Special paint; cleaner suitable for treated and untreated surfaces

Wallglaze Ltd
430 Kingstanding Road
Birmingham B44 9SF
Telephone 021-373 1680
Special coatings and paints; cleaners suitable for treated or untreated surfaces

Stainless steel sanitary ware

Concentric (Fabrications) Ltd
Unit 4, Hawksworth
Swindon, Wiltshire SN2 1DZ
Telephone Swindon 36756

W & G Sissons Ltd
Calver Mill, Calver Bridge
Sheffield S30 1XA
Telephone 0433 30791

Jumbo-sized lavatory rolls

Industrial Cleaning Papers Ltd
Manchester House, Church Way
Church Stretton, Salop
Telephone Church Stretton 3220

Anti-vandal lifts

Bennie Lifts Ltd
Tinworth Street
Albert Embankment
London SE11 5EJ
Telephone 01-735 2875

Wm Wadsworth & Sons Ltd
Lift Engineers
High Street
Bolton
Telephone Bolton 32811

Anti-vandal lift button system

Dewhurst & Partner Ltd
Melbourne Works
Inverness Road
Hounslow, Middlesex
Telephone 01-570 7791

Checklist of the Consortium for Method Building

Education building consortium comprising the County Councils of Berkshire, Cornwall, Devon, Northamptonshire, Oxfordshire, Somerset and Wiltshire.

	Likely damage	Remedy or precaution
ROOFS		
Roof generally	Damage by unauthorised traffic.	Make roof inaccessible, avoiding projections providing a climbing hold.
Finish	Chippings placed in RWP and hopper head outlets, causing blockages.	Make roof inaccessible.
Flashings	Removal of flashings with high scrap value.	Avoid lead and any similar 'valuable' materials.
Rooflights	Removal of rooflight glazing clips.	Ensure firm (screw) fixing and good quality clips.
	Breakage of rooflight glazing and resultant personal injuries.	Specify Georgian wired glass, or polycarbonate glass substitute.
RWPs	Ripping off by pulling or climbing.	Fix tight against wall if no RWP decoration necessary, to make unclimbable, or use anti-vandal paint.
	Breakage of downpipes: 1 PVC can be cut. 2 Asbestos is brittle; can be smashed. 3 Light steel and aluminium are easily crushed.	Specify best possible quality: medium-weight steel best.
CEILINGS		
Suspended ceilings	Entry via ceiling void to other rooms holding valuable equipment or allowing pilfering. Also panels displaced by articles thrown against them, and tiles and grid broken. Light fittings and conduit damaged. Non-replacement of tiles is a potential fire hazard.	Provide restricted access; clip down all lay-in tiles with non-removable clips where service access is not likely to be required. Avoid brittle tile types.
EXTERNAL WALLS		
External wall finishes	Pencil, Biro and aerosol graffiti.	Use roughcast surfaces to deter Biro or pencil users, or hard smooth finishes cleanable by solvent. Avoid siting 'writing' areas in places likely to be hidden or unsupervised. All surfaces are vulnerable to aerosols – cheap easily renewed surfaces may be preferred.
Applied claddings	Impact damage or deliberate removal in easily accessible areas, eg by entrances, footpaths, in playground areas.	Avoid thin or brittle materials eg asbestos-cement sheets, and tile hanging or slates (which can be used as instruments for further vandalism).
Flashings	See under Roofs.	
Doors generally	Removal by brute force; swinging on door where purchase is available.	Robust construction; ensure adequate hinge specification (size, material, strength and fixings). Avoid potential leverage points. Stops or buffers best sited opposite point of maximum leverage, eg opposite handle on wall.
	Hollow core stoved in.	Use kick plates and/or solid core.
	Impact damage by goods, trolleys, etc.	Suitably positioned protective plates.

Likely damage	Remedy or precaution

EXTERNAL WALLS

	Likely damage	Remedy or precaution
Door frames	Tearing of frame by attempted or complete removal of door.	Good quality timber of sufficiently robust section. Hinges as above.
Door observation panels	Breakage (and injury to person causing damage).	Avoid low-level glazing and use at least one cross rail in large glazed areas. Adequate specification; limit size for relative strength. NB: see also Internal walls: Doors.
Door louvres	Vulnerable to breakage.	Avoid use in accessible or potentially unsupervised areas.
Door ironmongery	Closers ripped off. Lever handles provide potential leverage. NB: persistent damage to doors has been overcome in some cases by reversing the hanging side.	Robust specification (not domestic quality). Use knob fittings to avoid leverage points (not in old people's homes).
Windows	Opening lights removed by leverage.	Ensure adequate frame and opening light sections and adequate size, material, strength and fixings for hinges.
Window ironmongery	Removal or breakage of fastenings.	Ensure good quality, adequate fixings with minimum potential leverage.
Window glazing	Breakage (by accident, including wind pressure, as well as vandalism).	Limit pane size and avoid siting at low levels or where exposed to potential hazards (eg entrances, ball games areas), or protect with rails.
	Injury to person causing damage and/or bystanders.	Use correct glass thickness in relation to pane size (CP 152 : 1972). Consider virtually unbreakable substitutes eg Plexiglas, Oroglas, Lexan (drawbacks: scratchable, poor fire performance, liability to bow and discolour, expensive – need to identify for firemen requiring access through windows). Possibly substitute solid panels in lieu of glass in persistent cases of vandalism. *NB: ease of replacement* 1 Consider access, avoiding outside scaffolding if possible, and allow for easy removal of associated internal fitments. Consider reversible opening lights which can be reglazed from inside. 2 Ensure manufacturers' reglazing literature available for proprietary opening lights. 3 Use simply withdrawable but burglar-proof gaskets. 4 Laminated glass is cheaper in terms of overall reglazing costs – can be cut from sheet, avoiding delay and temporary boarding up while awaiting toughened glass.
Window louvres	Removal or breakage of glass louvres.	Avoid siting in potentially unsupervised areas (screened off areas at ground-floor level) or accessible roofs.
	Personal injuries.	Ensure louvre type holds glass securely at all times.
Flue access	Inspection plates removed by fixing screw removal.	Phillips screw heads frustrate removal by coins and penknives.
Balanced flues	Wire guards flattened or damaged.	Ensure robust guards.

Likely damage	Remedy or precaution

INTERNAL WALLS NB: brick or block preferred

	Likely damage	Remedy or precaution
Partitions generally	Projecting surfaces (eg lippings) ripped off.	Avoid projections.
Lightweight partitions	Stoved in, or board finishes cracked, dented or cut.	Generally aim at robust construction. Avoid single plasterboard skin; use double skins. Ensure adequate studs at recommended centres. Avoid surfaces liable to fracture. Allow for ease of replacement in whole or part.
Fittings on lightweight partitions	Removal of fittings and support noggings causing extensive damage.	Provide adequate noggings positively secured to studs, and robust fixing of fitting to noggings.
WC cubicles	Extremities of panel vulnerable.	Metal channel trim preferred to applied edging in laminates.
	Junction with main enclosing walls vulnerable – gaps provide leverage.	Continuous channel fixing ('F' section) preferable to cleats at intervals.
	Swinging on fascia rail over doors; removal of doors.	Robust construction and fixings – adequate supervision.
Cubicle fittings	Unscrewed and removed, or ripped off.	Toilet roll holders etc back to back with bolt-through fixings and captive spindles. Isolated fittings (hooks etc) fixed with Phillips screws, or screw slot defaced as second preference.
	Knobs removed from indicator and other bolts.	Avoid screw-in fittings.
Internal wall decorations	Defacement and graffiti.	Any durable, washable surface, including appropriate paints. Tiling is impervious. Textured surfaces discourage graffiti but are bad for aerosol removal. Avoid wallpapers, except in adult or constantly supervised areas.
Doors	See under: External walls NB: note that use of observation panels (even obscured glazed) to toilet areas helps psychological control of vandalism by users.	
Internal glazing	Breakage causing personal injuries.	Adequate bedding and suitable surrounds; limit pane size, and do not use (or adequately protect) at low level to prevent 'walking through'. Use safety glass up to min. 1m above floor level.

FLOORS

	Likely damage	Remedy or precaution
Floor coverings	Carpet tiles removable.	Use semi-adhesive pads or avoid in high risk areas.
	Vinyl sheets and tiles defaced and burnt with cigarettes.	Fix sheet materials firmly at edges and weld seams. Ensure good adhesion for tiles. Use cigarette-proof quality.

STAIRCASES

	Likely damage	Remedy or precaution
Stairs, steps, handrails	Handrails and fixings vulnerable. Open wells prone to objects being dropped to bottom floor (or on to users' heads).	Ensure robust fixing and detail. In extreme cases consider netting in stairwells.

FIXTURES, FITTINGS etc

	Likely damage	Remedy or precaution
Cloakroom fittings	Hooks pulled from walls.	Use simply designed robust hooks within minimum leverage potential, and firmly fix.
Lockers	Chipboard units prone to splitting at hinges and other screw fittings – screws have low pull-out resistance in chipboard.	Blockboard preferred to chipboard for strength in use.
Fixings generally	Inadequate fixings allow easy removal of units from walls, doors and hinges etc.	Screw lengths for fixing wall units in particular should be clearly and adequately specified.

Likely damage	Remedy or precaution

SANITARY INSTALLATIONS

	Likely damage	Remedy or precaution
Toilet seats	Loosened or removed and stolen.	Strongest possible fittings, without lids, fixed with lock and not wing nuts.
Toilet pans	Can be completely removed and smashed. Pan ledges encourage collection of filth from deliberate actions.	Fix to floor with defaced brass screws. Avoid pan designs with ledges and crannies.
	Deliberate blocking of pans.	Rodding eyes on every pan and a simple fitting-to-manhole drain layout.
Flush pipe/drain connection	Rubber or pvc connectors easily slashed, leading to flooding.	Secure flush pipes with jubilee clips; drain connectors to be of robust material.
WC cisterns	Broken from their fixings.	Bolt fix through wall with spreader plates or large washers.
	Lids removed, overflow and valve tampered with to overflow on to seat (by removing medallion from hole provided for alternative lever handle). Filling of cistern, eg with paper or sanitary towels.	Site cistern at such a height as to make lid removal difficult, or place outside WC compartments with remote control operation.
WC chains	CP chain and handle broken or removed.	Substitute stout galvanised steel chain with pvc pull handle.
WC overflows	Source of various forms of damage resulting in flooding, which is particularly disastrous on upper floors.	Best solution is to discharge directly outside in an inaccessible position. Avoid discharging over pan or between seat and pan. Internally, if essential, use heavy gauge metal firmly fixed to walls, discharging over urinal channel.
Urinals	Pod urinals wrenched from walls, with fittings.	Firm fixings with non-plastic wastes. Stall urinals ideally in stainless steel preferred.
Sparge pipes	Blocking or drilled to drench the user. Tampering with flushing devices.	Conceal. Avoid screw-on outlet roses. Site outside the compartment or protect with strong wire cages.
Wash basins	Wrenched from walls by standing or sitting on basin lips, or levering from side to side.	Avoid siting beneath windows (inherent temptation to be used as platform to view passers-by). Support basin on dual or central bracket plus metal legs. Bolt brackets through wall with spreader plates. Bolt legs to floor, and use welded support framework.
	Removal of plugs and chains, with resultant blockage by paper towel makeshift 'plugs'.	Use captive plugs.
	Overflows blocked with paper.	Best avoided, as overflows can seldom cope with determined attempts to flood the lavatory compartment.
Basin wastes	Pvc is easily dismantled; bottle traps can be unscrewed and wastes blocked. Pvc generally can be burnt, kicked and climbed upon and fractured. Rodding eyes at run ends can be unscrewed.	Avoid bottle traps, especially to individual basins in a range. Substitute straight metal wastes discharging into open floor channel which drains whole compartment.
Basin services	Combinations of waste and hot and cold services liable to damage through inadequate fixing.	Screen services behind panels, or supply blended water in single, low pressure warm supply with all metal non-concussive taps.
	Cut-off valves and blenders can be tampered with.	Where exposure is unavoidable, use key operated valves.
Drinking fountains	Subject to breakage, removal and 'spraying' of adjacent areas by fingers placed on the jet.	Site in prominent positions. Stainless steel one-piece concealed control models offer best performance against vandalism.
Fixings generally	Wood plugs dry out and can be removed with their attached fitting. Similarly some	Use pipe brackets at 450mm max centres, fixed metal sleeve plugs or Rawlbolts.

Likely damage		Remedy or precaution

SANITARY INSTALLATIONS

Fixings generally	pvc wallplugs will not grip in certain blocks.	Deface screw-heads or use anti-theft screws.
	NB: most damage to sanitary equipment and services can result in flooding causing widespread damage. Floors should be designed with falls towards gulleys or channels (see Basin wastes above), also aiding general cleaning operations.	

SITE FURNITURE AND SURFACE COVERINGS etc

Gates	Can be stood upon, swung on and deformed or lifted from hinges, damaged or stolen.	Reduce leverage points to minimum and use non lift-off hinges.
Fences	Chain link can be cut, standards bent and line wires removed or seriously distorted.	Use galvanised tubular supports in preference to angle. Gravel boards can receive link fixings at the fence base. Line wires 75mm from top, not through top links. Use adequate (10g) galvanised link – not plastic covered.
	Interwoven panels subject to breakage.	Not recommended – vertical boarding possible alternative (expensive).
Walls	Copings can be lifted off and used as weapons for future damage.	Double bullnose brick on edge.
	Movement off dpc by impact.	Omit dpc for freestanding playwalls etc; instead use engineering brick or similar.
Surfaces	Gravel paths provide 'ammunition' for damage; can block gulleys, etc.	Avoid if possible.
	Pebbles or cobbles can be removed and used for further damage.	Ensure at least two-thirds depth of pebbles etc set into bedding.

DRAINAGE

	Gulley grids which are removable allow for potential drain blockages, often by gravel.	Use lock down gulley grids (applies equally to rodding eye covers).

HEATING, MECHANICAL & ELECTRICAL SERVICES

Fan convectors	Casings broken, partly dismantled; motors removed, grilles deformed.	Avoid or use recessed type. Specify more robust grilles.
Wall thermostats	Damaged beyond repair. Prone to tampering. Wires pulled out.	Avoid in exposed positions wherever possible, or build into convectors.
Electrical appliances generally	Wires pulled out and cable stripped bare. Fuses removed.	Use central distribution boards in lockable cupboards. Avoid local fusing, eg in classrooms.
Lighting fittings generally	Breakage.	Consider non-glass diffusers.
Fluorescent fittings	End caps and starter motors removed.	Use recessed fluorescent fittings – quick start type needs no motor.
External lights	Glassware broken.	Care required in siting and specification.
Socket outlets	Shorted out or blocked up.	Shuttered outlets may slightly reduce incidence; vandal-resistant types now available.
Shower spray heads	Adjustable heads particularly vulnerable to breakage and removal.	More robust fixed head types preferable.
Oil tank gauges	See-through gauges on external tanks broken or bent over to syphon out oil.	Site in adequately supervised areas, or in boiler houses.
Valves generally	Unauthorised operation.	Use lockshield type or conceal or protect.
Water stopcocks	Unauthorised operation.	Place in pits, preferably with key operated cover.
Copper piping	Can be flattened or joints pulled apart.	Concealed pipe runs or protection by casing.

Short bibliography

(see also the bibliographical notes to the sections)

Association of London Borough Housing Managers (ALBHM): *Vandalism and Policing on Housing Estates*, The Association (London 1973)

Clarke, R V G (ed): *Tackling Vandalism*, HMSO (London 1978)

Clinard, M B and Wade, A: 'Towards the delineation of vandalism as a subtype in juvenile delinquency', *Journal of Criminal Law*, no 48 pp 493-499

Cohen, S: 'The politics of vandalism', *New Society*, 12 December 1966

Cohen, S: 'The nature of vandalism', *New Society*, 12 December 1966

Cohen, S: 'Can it be controlled?', *New Society*, 12 December 1966

Department of the Environment: *Wilful Damage on Housing Estates*, Building Research Station Digest no 132 (London 1971)

Design Bulletin: *Children at Play*, Design Bulletin no 27, HMSO (London 1973)

Freeman, L: 'The face of vandalism', *Municipal Journal*, 13 July 1975

Goldman, N: 'A socio-psychological study of school vandalism', *Crime and Delinquency*, vol 7, 1961, pp 221-230

Greenberg, B: *School Vandalism a National Dilemma*, Stanford Research Institute (California 1969)

Henderson, M: 'Gibbshill boys', *New Society*, 15 July 1976

Home Office: *Protection against Vandalism*, Report of Home Office Standing Committee on Crime Prevention, HMSO (London 1975)

Jacobs, J: *The Death and Life of Great American Cities*, Random House (New York 1961). Published Penguin Books (Harmondsworth 1965)

Madison, A: *Vandalism: the Not-so-senseless Crime*, Seabury Press (New York 1970)

Marshall, T: 'Vandalism: the seeds of destruction', *New Society*, 17 June 1976

Martin, J M: *Juvenile Vandalism*, Charles C Thomas (Springfield, Illinois 1961)

Mayhew, P M, Clarke, R V G, Sturman, A and Hough, J M: 'Damage on buses: the effects of supervision' in *Crime as Opportunity*, Home Office Research Study no 34, HMSO (London 1976)

Municipal Journal: 'One city's approach to security' *Municipal Journal*, vol 80 no 23, 9 June 1972, pp 807-811

Newman, O: *Defensible Space*, Architectural Press (London 1973)

Olson, H C and Carpenter, J B: *A Survey of Techniques Used to Reduce Vandalism and Delinquency in Schools*, Research Analysis Corporation (Virginia 1971)

Pablant, P and Baxter, J C: 'Environmental correlates of school vandalism' *Journal of American Institute of Planners*, no 241, 1975, pp 270-279

Prewer, R R: 'Some observations on window-smashing', *British Journal of Delinquency*, no 10, 1959, pp 104-113

Pullen, D: 'Memoirs of vandalism', *New Society*, 6 February 1975

Shelter: 'Vandalism: Hounslow Council', *Shelter Information Bulletin*, 3-9 June 1976

Spence, J and Hedges, A: *Community Planning Project: Cunningham Road Improvement Scheme Interim Report*, Social and Community Planning Research, Barry Rose (Publishers) (Chichester 1976)

Stove, J and Taylor, F (eds): *Vandalism in Schools*, Save the Children, February 1977

Wallis, H F: 'The roots and fruits of vandalism', *Municipal Review*, no 549, September 1975

Ward, A: 'Social processes in the act of juvenile vandalism' in Clinard, M B and Quinney, R (eds): *Criminal Behaviour Systems*, Holt, Rinehart and Winston (New York 1967)

Ward, C (ed): *Vandalism*, Architectural Press (London 1973)

Acknowledgements

The Design Council would like to thank The Architectural Press Ltd for permission to quote from *Vandalism* edited by Colin Ward, and *New Society* for permission to quote from 'Vandalism: the seeds of destruction' by T Marshall which first appeared in *New Society*, London, the weekly review of the social sciences.

The photograph on page 70 is crown copyright. Reproduced from Digest 132 by permission of the Director, Building Research Establishment.

Index

Names and titles from the bibliography and references are
not indexed unless they also occur in the text